POPULATION GROWTH— THREAT TO PEACE?

POPULATION GROWTH—THREAT TO PEACE?

A *Wisdom and Discovery Book*

Under the theme "Wisdom and Discovery for a Dynamic World," Georgetown University marked the 175th anniversary of her founding in 1789 with a varied program of lectures, conferences, and symposia on key ideas and issues of our time. From the addresses and deliberations on these occasions have come the volumes being published as WISDOM AND DISCOVERY BOOKS.

The present volume consists of the papers of the 37th Annual Conference of the Catholic Association for International Peace, held in Washington, D. C., on October 22–25, 1964, in conjunction with the 175th anniversary observance of Georgetown University.

RILEY HUGHES
General Editor

POPULATION GROWTH— THREAT TO PEACE?

Edited by WILLIAM E. MORAN, JR.

GEORGE H. DUNNE, S.J.   ·   OSCAR HARKAVY

GEORGE N. SHUSTER   ·   BERNARD BERELSON

CALVERT L. DEDRICK   ·   RICHARD N. GARDNER

IRENE B. TAEUBER   ·   WILLIAM E. MORAN, JR.

JOHN L. THOMAS, S.J.   ·   ROBERT F. DRINAN, S.J.

TERRENCE J. MURPHY

A Wisdom and Discovery Book

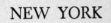

P. J. KENEDY & SONS   ·   NEW YORK

CONTENTS

5

NOTES ON CONTRIBUTORS

WILLIAM E. MORAN, JR., is dean of the School of Foreign Service, Georgetown University, and president of the Catholic Association for International Peace. He is an alumnus of Syracuse University and the Syracuse University College of Law. His experience in public administration includes service in the Federal Bureau of Investigation, Department of State, Atomic Energy Commission, Marshall Plan Mission, Mutual Security Administration, and Foreign Operations Administration. He is a former director of the Africa Research Program, Stanford Research Institute, and a board member of the Population Reference Bureau and the Institute for Human Progress.

GEORGE H. DUNNE, S. J., is assistant to the president of Georgetown University for International Programs. A graduate of Loyola and Gonzaga universities, he earned his Ph.D. in international relations at the University of Chicago. He has taught at St. Louis University, Loyola University, and the University of Santa Clara, and has written numerous articles on social, racial, and political problems. He is the author of *Generation of Giants* and the editor of *Poverty in Plenty*, a WISDOM AND DISCOVERY BOOK.

GEORGE N. SHUSTER is assistant to the president of the University of Notre Dame. An alumnus of Notre Dame, he also studied at the University of Poitiers and earned his Ph.D. at Columbia University. The author of fifteen books, he was formerly chairman of the English department at Notre Dame, managing editor of *The Commonweal*, a fellow of the Social Science Research Council, and president of Hunter College. He has served as Land Commissioner for Bavaria and as United States

7

Representative on the executive board of UNESCO. A former president of the Catholic Association for International Peace, he is a trustee of the Carnegie Endowment for International Peace.

CALVERT LAMPERT DEDRICK has been chief of the international statistical programs of the Bureau of the Census since 1946. After receiving his Ph.D. in 1933 from the University of Wisconsin, he served as consultant to the Unemployment Census and to the Department of Justice. A member of the Statistical Mission to Japan in 1951 and to Lebanon in 1954, he has served as United States delegate to many international statistics conferences, including the World Population Conference in Rome in 1954 and the ECAFE statistics conference in Bangkok in 1956 and 1960.

IRENE BARNES TAEUBER is a senior research demographer in the Office of Population Research, Princeton University. A graduate of the University of Missouri and Northwestern University, she received her Ph.D. from the University of Minnesota. She has done extensive population study and consultation abroad, notably in Japan, the Philippines, Thailand, Pakistan, and the USSR. In 1964 she was a member and *rapporteur* of the United Nations Economic and Social Council. The author of some two hundred technical articles, she has also written *The Future Population of Europe and the Soviet Union, Public Health and Demography in the Far East,* and *The Population of Japan.*

JOHN L. THOMAS, S. J., is an associate professor of sociology at St. Louis University. An alumnus of Loras College, St. Louis University, and the University of Montreal, he received his Ph.D. in sociology from the University of Chicago. He has been a member of the Institute of Social Order since 1949. His books include *The American Catholic Family,* which received the Catholic Sociological Society Award for 1956; *Marriage and Rhythm; Catholic Viewpoint on Marriage and the Family;* and *Religion and the American People.*

OSCAR HARKAVY, director of the population program of The Ford Foundation, is in charge of grant-making on a world-wide basis in reproductive biology, demography, and other fields. A graduate of Columbia University, from 1946 to 1953 he taught finance, insurance, and statistics at Syracuse University, where he had earned an M.B.A. in finance and a Ph.D. in economics. He is a member of the American Economic Association, American Finance Association, and Population Association of America.

BERNARD BERELSON is vice president of the Population Council. An alumnus of Whitman College and the University of Washington, he received his Ph.D. from the University of Chicago, where he subsequently taught and served as dean of the Graduate Library School. He formerly was research director of the Bureau of Applied Social Research, Columbia University, and director of the behavioral sciences program of The Ford Foundation. His books include *The Behavioral Sciences Today* and (with Gary A. Steiner) *Human Behavior: An Inventory of Scientific Findings*.

RICHARD N. GARDNER is Deputy Assistant Secretary of State for International Organization Affairs. A graduate of Harvard University and the Yale University Law School, he received his Ph.D. in 1954 from Oxford University, where he was a Rhodes Scholar. A former professor of law at Columbia University, he is the author of *Sterling-Dollar Diplomacy*, *New Directions in U. S. Foreign Economic Policy*, and *In Pursuit of World Order*. A member of the Council on Foreign Relations, he was appointed by President Johnson as a member of the United States Delegation to the United Nations General Assembly.

ROBERT F. DRINAN, S. J., is dean and professor of law of the Boston College Law School. A graduate of Boston College, he received his LL.B. and LL.M. from Georgetown University. He is vice president of the Massachusetts Bar Association, chairman of an advisory committee to the United States Commission on Civil

Rights, and a member of the national executive committee of
the American Judicature Society. A contributor to law journals
and other periodicals, he is a corresponding editor of *America*
and the author of *Religion, the Courts and Public Policy*.

TERRENCE J. MURPHY is executive vice president of the College of
St. Thomas, St. Paul, Minnesota. A graduate of St. Paul Semi-
nary and the University of Minnesota, he received his Ph.D. in
political science from Georgetown University. He served as a
United States Air Force chaplain from 1949 to 1954 and is
now the chaplain for the 934th Troop Carrier Group. He is a
member of the board of governors of the national office of the
Catholic Association for International Peace. In 1960 and 1961
he received grants from the Hill Foundation for research in the
field of civil liberties. He is the author of *Censorship, Government and Obscenity*.

INTRODUCTION

WILLIAM E. MORAN, JR.

The Catholic Association for International Peace has for thirty-seven years been studying problems related to peace in the world from a Christian standpoint. It has provided a forum for Catholic scholars interested in such issues. Its annual conference has traditionally explored in some depth an issue of current importance.

In preparing for the 37th Annual Conference, it was decided that rapid population growth in the world was an issue of critical importance and should be considered as a topic of the conference. Once the idea was broached there was little difficulty in seeing the necessity for its consideration by such a group. It was clear in the fall of 1963, when our discussions began, that this was a critical issue to which our society was going to have to address itself. While it was apparent that the problem was highly complex and involved much more than birth control or the acceptability of a particular method, it was also true that many Catholics were hampered in discussing the issue, if not actually silenced, because of difficulty they faced in reconciling the position of their Church on contraception with the views of many of those involved in the discussion. Yet Catholics must involve themselves, since the decisions made and the actions taken will have serious implications for them and their society. The association was in a position to bring this to their attention, along with material geared to

11

informing them of the problem and acceptable approaches to it, on the basis of which they might become capable of preparing themselves for effective participation in discussions and decisions on the various issues involved.

Georgetown University was engaged in celebrating its 175th Anniversary under the theme, "Wisdom and Discovery for a Dynamic World." Here was an area where wisdom and discovery were patently needed. Georgetown had already established a Population Research Center; it is, in fact, the first Catholic university in this country to have done so. The association asked for and received the University's cosponsorship for this endeavor.

Thanks are due to the Program Committee of the Catholic Association for International Peace, which, under my chairmanship, consisted of Benedict Duffy, M.D., Victor Ferkiss, Right Reverend Monsignor Joseph Gremillion, John T. Miller, Jr., and Reverend James L. Vizzard, S.J., and to the Reverend George Dunne, S.J., of Georgetown University, for developing the program for the conference. Particular thanks are due to the participants for the way in which they responded to our efforts and the character of their presentations.

In a brief space of time, just a very few years, important segments of our society here at home and of those involved in the development process abroad have come to realize that rapid rates of population growth present serious problems. Many insist that after the problem of nuclear warfare, the problem of population is the most important one facing mankind in our age.

There is a tendency on the part of many to see rapid rates of population growth as giving rise to a barrier on the road to progress and threatening peace and stability in the world because population growth may make it impossible to meet in a timely fashion the reasonable aspirations of hundreds of millions of peoples in the underdeveloped countries. There is a tendency to move from this conclusion, in an age where science and technology have largely replaced recourse to magic and miracles, to the belief that all that is needed is the development and distribution of cheap and effective contraceptive devices. From this it is but a short step to the belief that all that stands in the way of an effective program of this nature is the Catholic Church with its continued refusal to accept the use of artificial devices to inhibit contraception.

Still others, with a similar faith in science and technology, insist that the Malthusians and neo-Malthusians are wrong, and that there is no population problem. They believe that there are adequate resources in the world and a sufficiently developed technology for it to be possible to feed an ever-increasing number throughout the world for decades to come. The problem is not so simple. While, in theory, the resources may exist and the technology may be available, the fact is that already with the growth of population in this century one to one and one-half billion people are hungry. And this is speaking at the animal level. This takes no account of the lost dignity for the man who cannot for lack of education and means realize his potential or see the hope that his children may realize theirs. Even now we face a grave problem arising from population growth which has already taken place. As one of our contributors points out, something like one-third of the population which will inhabit the earth by 1980 is already born. The same contributor also points out that, even if the most sanguine hopes of those who propose birth control as a solution were realized, the populations of Latin America and South Asia would still double before the end of the century.

We are faced with the problem of rapid population growth because of the wonders science and technology have made possible. We have been able cheaply and effectively to reduce the death rate throughout the world. We are now faced with quite a different kind of problem. If significant reductions are to be made in birth rates, or if there are to be significant increases in production and distribution of food and other goods in the world, much will have to be done by hundreds of millions of people throughout the earth. No external agency can do it for them, as it could in controlling death rates. Yet these people, in the main unlettered and living in traditional societies, are antipathetic if not antithetic to the acceptance of new ways or the applications of new methods made possible by science and technology. Great social change, which we barely begin to know how to bring about, or to cope with, will be required if we are to begin to solve this population problem in this century.

In general terms, it may well be true that there are adequate resources in the world and a sufficient knowledge of technology that it would be possible, not alone to feed the world's population, but to meet the minimum needs for human life and dignity throughout the planet. If true, it is so only in global terms. The resources themselves and the people with the knowledge and willingness to apply the skills are not evenly distributed nor will they be at any early date. Despite the willingness of wealthy countries with surplus food supplies to cooperate in a Food for Peace program, there have been distinct limits as to the ability to use surplus foods in many areas because adequate distribution systems were not available. There is a reasonable question as to how long the wealthy countries will be prepared to use their resources and skills to compensate for inadequacies in the poorer countries.

The problems presented by rapid population growth are many and complex, and we shall be grappling with them for decades to come. If we do not deal with them effectively and in a timely fashion, they may well threaten the tranquillity, even the peace of the world. More than this, for those who profess Christianity, this is a moral problem of awesome dimensions.

It has been our effort in this discussion to make a first step in identifying some of the main issues involved and suggesting questions requiring urgent attention. It is our hope that this first step may lead many to think, study, and act.

A Word on Objectives

George H. Dunne, S.J.

The extraordinarily rapid increase of the world population constitutes a serious problem to which no citizen of the world can remain indifferent. In his great encyclical *Mater et Magistra,* Pope John XXIII clearly defined the nature of the problem:

> Looking at the question on a world-wide scale, some consider that, according to sufficiently reliable statistics, the human race, in a few decades, will experience a notable increase in numbers, while the rate of economic growth will be considerably slower. Some take this to mean that unless something is done to check population growth, the lack of balance between size of population and the means of subsistence will make itself felt more acutely in the not-too-distant future.
>
> It is clear that in the less-developed nations—still relying on statistical data—the rapid spread of modern hygienic methods and medical remedies reduces the death rate among infants, and thus lengthens the life span. At the same time, the number of births, where it is now normally high, tends to remain more or less constant, at least for a considerable period of time. But, while the number of births exceeds the number of deaths in the same year, the productive efficiency of the respective economic systems does not increase proportionately. Accordingly, an improvement in the standard of living in these underdeveloped states is almost impossible. Indeed, it is rather inevitable that things will get worse. . . .

As Pope John XXIII pointed out, there are two aspects of the problem:

(1) The long-range question of whether the potential resources of the world will prove inadequate to support the world population.

(2) The immediate problem of underdeveloped countries, where the inadequacy of actually available resources is already demonstrated and where population growth advances at such a rate as to outstrip any possible expansion of resources.

With respect to the long-range question, the Pope states that the available data are still too uncertain and incomplete to permit a certain answer one way or the other. Nearly all experts will agree with this. As for the other and immediate problem of the underdeveloped countries, the Pope frankly recognizes its existence: "We appreciate the fact," he wrote, "that in certain underdeveloped areas and states, serious problems and difficulties of this nature can and do present themselves."

Beyond insisting that the solution must not be sought by recourse to contraception and a general admonition that "the solution is to be found only in socioeconomic progress achieved in a moral atmosphere . . . [and] must also embrace world-wide cooperation that permits and favors an orderly and fruitful international exchange of useful knowledge," the Pope made no concrete suggestions about how the problem is to be met.

The remarks of Pope John XXIII both explain and justify the selection of this subject by the Catholic Association for International Peace as the theme of this discussion. The problem exists. It is serious. It affects the common good of the world community. It must, therefore, concern us as citizens of the world.

The main preoccupation of our organization, as its title suggests, is with peace, which is an order of justice. The pressure of rapid population growth tends to nullify, as Pope John remarked, all efforts to establish an order of justice in underdeveloped areas of the world, notably in Latin America and in India, to cite conspicuous examples, and consequently constitutes a threat to world peace.

A further reason for our interest in the subject is that ours is a Catholic organization. To many it seems that the Church, by virtue of the position she holds—or, more exactly, perhaps, the position she is commonly, though erroneously, thought to hold—with respect to birth control, is a major obstacle to an effective attack upon this problem. This, I think, imposes upon us, especially since we live in a pluralistic society, the obligation (1) to clarify our position, first to ourselves and then to those who hold other opinions, and (2) to seek rational solutions consistent with the requirements of the moral order. Otherwise, we should appear to be negative obstructionists, indifferent to the critical problems of overpopulation, undernourishment, and large-scale human suffering.

I mentioned the need to clarify the Catholic position first to ourselves. This is important, because, unless I am much mistaken, Catholics are not always correctly informed either about the position taken by the Church or about the precise reasons for that position. Thus some labor under the misapprehension that the Church is adamantly opposed to any control of marital procreative activity. She is not. She is, of course, opposed to methods of birth control which in her judgment violate the natural law. For this reason she is opposed to abortion and to infanticide, two methods of birth control which have often been, and still are, resorted to by men. She has also opposed the use of mechanical instruments which by intervening in the sex act itself destroy the integrity of the act by preventing it from proceeding to its appointed end. The end of a thing being its nature, as Aristotle re-marked, such intervention, being against the end of the act, is therefore against its nature. Unless I am mistaken, this is the philosophical basis of the Church's position. It is not that such a practice is against the nature of marriage, as I have heard some say, but that it is against the nature of the act itself. I think the distinction most important and believe that it may have a bearing upon the search for morally acceptable methods of contraceptive control.

It may be, of course, that in the search for morally ac-ceptable solutions we may discover that the only answer to the problem is self-control and self-denial. If this be so, then we should know it and assume the staggering responsibility of devising methods to develop self-control and self-denial on the part of the teeming millions of potential progenitors.

It may be that the answer is to be found, if I may be crudely prosaic about it, in more fertilizer. If this is the case, we should know it and concern ourself with producing more fertilizer. It may be that the answer is to be sought in less fertility. If that is the case, we should know it and concern ourselves with how to reduce fertility without violating the order of nature.

These remarks should not be understood in a literal sense. What I am saying is simply that there is a problem, and that it is, therefore, entirely appropriate, perhaps singularly appro-priate, for Catholics to be concerned about it.

There is, of course, no single and no simple solution to this extremely complex problem. To make the mistake of acting upon the assumption that there is may seriously threaten some of the principal foundation stones of human society.

The Catholic Association for International Peace is fully aware of this. It did not organize this discussion under the illusion that it would discover a solution. Its scope is much less

ambitious. It hopes to broaden our understanding of the
dimensions of the problem; perhaps to suggest certain avenues
which should be explored in seeking solutions; possibly to
identify other suggested avenues as moral, or psychological, or
sociological cul-de-sacs, leading nowhere. It also hopes, I
should think, that among its fruits will be a larger Catholic
participation in the search for right answers.

Population Growth—Field for Study

George N. Shuster

Three years ago we began at Notre Dame to ask the question: what should a university like ours undertake in this field of study? In order to find out we have since staged three major conferences as well as a number of more informal ones. The major ones enlisted a formidable array of demographers, sociologists, jurists, and theologians. We also took a good, hard look at what the biologists, notably those concerned with ecology, had to say on the subject. I cannot, unfortunately, report that we reached anything like a consensus—to borrow a word which I do not like. But we did agree about some things, and no doubt I might as well begin by enumerating these.

First, when we talk about the problem of population, we are not concerned with the special economic, psychological, biological, and moral difficulties which modern marriage brings with it. These difficulties are of course very grave, and they give the moralists in particular a hard time. Nothing I shall say could possibly make life any easier for them.

Second, it is doubtless true that the world would be much better off if it were populated by men and women whose spiritual insight and religious motivation were of a high order. This is the cardinal principle which determines the religious mission in all ages, and which we can only support as fervently and intelligently as possible. But since the human race is unfortunately not of the kind so described, we can only assume that it will act in this area as it does in others. That is, it will experiment; and eventually the state as the voice of the citizenry however constituted will intervene in one way or another to bring about results which seem to it desirable. Thus there would be no homicides if society were truly Christian. But there happen to be a great many homicides in this and other relatively barbarous countries. I do not believe that anybody is likely to prove conservative enough to turn this particular matter over to the individual citizen.

Third, the problem of population is not primarily one of the food supply. Of course it would be if the rate of increase continued indefinitely at the pace which is now observable in the Caribbean area, probably that in which the race is now procreating most exuberantly. But there is no reason to assume that in general the growth of population will not slow down or that the supply of food will not increase. Let us recall that some of the most eloquent demographers now living were alarmed in the days of their youth by the specter of population decline. All I myself have learned about the food problem is pretty well summarized in an article by Harvard's Jean Mayer, entitled "Food and Population: The Wrong Problem?" in the summer 1964 issue of *Daedalus*. Perhaps not all the cognoscenti will agree with Dr. Mayer's conclusions, but I am, after all, only reporting about my own education. He simply says that the quantities of food which might be produced are literally incalculable.

What we seem to have learned about the problem before us again boils down to three absorbing facts.

First, increases in population result from differences between the birth rate and the death rate. If the first is 50 per 1,000 and the second 40 per 1,000, the population increase will be 10 per 1,000. This sounds simple enough, but the more you look at it the more complex it becomes. Of all the points in the arc of human experience this is the one which science has most dramatically dislocated. As biology and medicine have advanced in the conquest of infection and disease, they have decreased the rate of infant mortality and lengthened the life-expectancy pattern. This means that the rate of population increase is potentially far, far greater now than it could have been in any previous period of history. Even more dramatic—one might even say melodramatic—is the decline in the rate of maternal deaths in childbirth. When I recall my own early years in Wisconsin it comes as quite a shock to realize how many such deaths there were and how often it happened that men would marry three or four times as a result. The psychological effects of such a situation were doubtless very great and may well have induced crude forms of birth prevention seldom talked about in those days.

This change in the dialogue between birth and death goes hand in hand with the other major alteration of human circumstance by science, namely industrialization. As long as a country is predominatingly rural it will be governed by the rhythm of rural life. That is, people will till the fields and raise livestock. As time goes on, provided there are neither wars nor plagues, there will be more human beings than the land and its products can support.

We can follow this very closely in the history of Europe. All the tillable soil except that owned by a relatively few manorial estates was gradually divided and subdivided until the individual parcels became too small to be viable bases from which to sustain family life. There sometimes followed a clamor to break up the manorial estates as well, but even then the net result was hardly more impressive than is the current addition to Egypt's arable land by reason of the building of the Aswan

Dam. More and more young people drifted to urban areas. Such were the people who manned the capitalist system in England, France, and Germany during the nineteenth century. Often they had a desperately hard time of it, one of the consequences of which was Marxism. But in the long run industry was able not only to absorb large numbers of workers under terms which were human but also to support welfare systems, of which the first—it is well to note—was established by that archenemy of what is today called "liberal thought," Prince Otto von Bismarck. Europe, it may be noted in passing, had adopted Medicare while we were still hunting buffalo.

Second, what one observes today in many troubled parts of the world is a situation having two prongs. First, there are agricultural areas from which there really is no place to go. One of these is Egypt, another Haiti. When one has seen the vast numbers of destitute, underfed, and diseased human beings who constitute the population in such countries, one has at least reckoned with some aspects of the problem in an offhand but still sobering way. I wish that everybody who, enjoying the benefits of middle-class culture in the United States, including a bathroom with hot and cold water on tap and a cocktail or two before dinner, still says that the population problem does not exist would go to Cairo and its environs and make a frank assessment of the human hopes and values of the people he encounters, and ask himself what he would do if he were one of them.

The second prong is the one which is currently so visible in Latin America. People—men, women, and children—crowd toward the cities from their impoverished and overcrowded rural areas. They build slum suburbs (one can see them in Turkey, too) out of primitive shacks—areas which have no water, plumbing, or electricity. These are not bad people, without intellectual or moral endowments. Indeed, walking about in some of the *barriadas* which surround Lima it is almost unbelievably pathetic to see that there are outposts of the city's banks—places where people deposit sols which they have somehow scraped together. The death rate is high but the crime rate is not.

Third, the principal problem, therefore, is: how can the European process be repeated in these situations? We must remember, first of all, that the rate of population growth in pre-capitalist Europe was lower, not being affected by modern medicine. Even so it was a serious enough state of affairs to disturb Malthus, a scrupulously moral person who advocated an extension of celibacy. Second, the tempo of industrial growth was stimulated by monopolies of a technological character. There was, for example, the British method of manufacturing steel, about which Krupp learned and created a great undertaking in the Ruhr. And finally there was emigration.

The problem of Latin America, as of Asia and the Near East, is how to industrialize without (a) the advantages of patents and processes, (b) without succumbing to competition, and (c) without surmounting the barrier of population increases. Of course the situation would doubtless be less trying than it now is if the rich of some countries had been less selfish and more enterprising. But this is like saying that Adolf Hitler would never have come to power if President von Hindenburg had acted differently. We have, perforce, to take our present stance in the present. The solution can no doubt be found without recourse to magic, and is, as a matter of fact, being found in some places. The approach to the solution is, of course, complicated by political instability. How fortunate we in the United States are to live in a political order which has its roots in the Anglo-Saxon tradition can hardly be grasped until one has been in some place where that tradition has no foundation.

At any rate, we shall now try to envisage the effect of population increases, though admittedly it is difficult to disentangle these from other factors. If we assume an increase in the output of the total economy of 10 per cent, this should mean that every citizen living by that economy has benefited, though perhaps not equally. But if the 10 per cent is offset by a comparable increase in the population, no generally noticeable improvement will have taken place. The situation will be far worse if the number of people grows larger while the output of the economy actually declines. Of course if the society is as affluent as ours is, population growth may be desirable. I am not arguing that it actually is, but the point at which disaster must set in may be relatively remote.

Let us consider some aspects of our economy which are not transferable to areas in process of development. With us, for example, education has become increasingly an instrument for lessening the impact of youth on the labor market. But education is a good thing—even a good thing to which, it may be, men and women have a kind of natural right. Therefore the fact that we have an industrial society which cannot absorb all the physically and mentally able into the work force early is beneficent because we can afford the cost—even if some people do not think so.

Or, again, we can use programs of public works to supplement industrial employment, and there are those who argue that this is precisely what an affluent society ought to do. But at the present time very few developing societies can manage anything of this kind. Almost everywhere people are caught in the vise of a dilemma which is cruel enough. On the one hand you cannot develop industry unless a relatively skilled work force is available. Yet such a force is unobtainable without training. How shall enough money be allocated from current income to meet the requirement of one sector without lessening what one can give to another?

What all this adds up to is that marked population increases of say 2.5 per cent may doom to poverty and its attendant ills, not only the newborn children, but their elders as well in not a few countries. This is hardly a statement anyone would make lightly, nor was it so made at any of the conferences held at Notre Dame or at the University of Louvain. What it implies is apparent. Governments affected by the situations described will attempt to do something about them. It is their problem and not ours. The United States should certainly not make population control a prerequisite for foreign aid. In so sensitive an area suggestions coming from this country are bound to seem culturally imperialistic. On the other hand, it is equally obvious that Catholic comment cannot ignore grim realities. A great deal of private experimenting with family limitation is going on in developing countries, and much of it cannot be contemplated without revulsion. The gamut from battered babies through abortion to infanticide is being traversed every day. But vastly more significant, no doubt, is that large numbers of children are born in absolute squalor, without being given the slightest chance to attain even to an absolute minimum of human decency. However resolutely we may define the moral teaching of the Church, it must always be conceded that this teaching presupposes ability to exercise judgment and to attain to spiritual motivation.

But what Catholics certainly can do—and what they too frequently shy away from—is to help improve as rapidly as possible the basic economic and social conditions which breed human despair. That changes for the better are daily being brought about in many parts of the world is a fact. Paul Hoffmann's *World Without Want* makes the point this way: "It will obviously take a long time, even in the most favorable circumstance, for any serious impact to be made on the problem of the excessively high rates of population increase. This makes all the more urgent the job of accelerating the pace of economic growth and social advancement in the underdeveloped world."

He goes on to show how this is possible, by describing what will happen when the new dam at Kainji, Nigeria, is completed through the good offices of the UN: "If the UN blueprint is followed, the scheme will permit hydroelectric power production at an installed capacity of 860 megawatts, 22 per cent more than the Grand Coulee—and substantially more than any dam in Western Europe. This is enough to satisfy the electricity requirements of Nigeria, so far as anyone can foresee them, for twenty years."

This is sufficient food for anybody's reflective digestion. If one can make any general criticism of Catholic attitudes on the problem as a whole it is this: we are very generous when it comes to thinking of the religious or indeed more generally the welfare needs of poorer peoples. The record of Catholic missions, and indeed of Protestant missions, too, is a glorious one. We set up schools and hospitals, rescue abandoned babies, send abroad priests, religious, and lay folk with prodigal charity. But we have not yet grown accustomed to recognizing that something like the introduction of hybrid corn can accomplish many thousand times more in terms of human well-being on this earth. We have not harnessed the sciences to our conception of service.

The idea thus expressed is of course not novel. I shall quote from a book by the Reverend Dr. Carl Sonnenschein, eminent and beloved Berlin Catholic theologian and sociologist, who was active during the period between the two wars:

I should be ashamed of myself were I to go about preaching the Ten Commandments in the northern and eastern sections of Berlin were I not at the same time to work as hard as possible to see that those Commandments can be obeyed. To advocate family life in which children are welcome is impossible unless one advocates at the same time continuous social reform. . . . The slums of the big city are areas from which Christian culture is kept by a blockade. The atmosphere of health and of Christian living is not to be found in damp flats and unlighted barracks. We are taught that the premiss of all supernatural life, of the life of grace, is the natural order. Therefore we must establish a new connection between religion and industrial activity. Therefore we must be interested in social welfare. Not as if it were a game. No, it is the never-ending duty of the whole people, especially of that part of it which believes in God.

Beyond any question, if more Germans had listened to Father Sonnenschein and followed his counsel they might have been spared the degradation of the twelve years of Hitler's Reich. Too many of us would not have done so either. We are now part way along in the history of the Development Decade, which President Kennedy inaugurated with so much spirit. Two things may be said about the methodology of the decade: first, it is a concerted effort by the United Nations and its specialized agencies to combat ignorance, poverty, and disease in what we choose to call the underdeveloped countries; and second, it is the endeavor of our country, seen as complementing the generosity of other countries, with bilateral programs. Now with the passing of time I have grown less and less eager to separate Catholics from other citizens of the country when there is a question of public policy, but it can do no great harm—indeed, it may accomplish a modest amount of good—to do so briefly on this occasion. Should we not candidly admit as Catholics that our knowledge and support of the United Nations and its specialized agencies are woefully limited, and that even the Foreign Aid program of the United States gets little recognizable support from us? I shall illustrate with a personal experience. No commercial is intended, and I shall add by way of preface that the Catholic press has been very kind to me. Recently, after a number of years of experience with the organization, I wrote a book about UNESCO. This has attracted notice in many distinguished journals here and abroad and has had some effect on public policy. But so far as I have been able to determine not a single line of comment has appeared in any American Catholic newspaper or magazine, exception having duly been made for a flyer distributed by a Los Angeles Catholic group. This accused me of ignorance, hostility to the Constitution, and several kinds of treason.

Now whether we like it or not UNESCO has become a powerful force in the development of education throughout the world. In addition to its own resources, it directs far-flung activities for the United Nations Technical Assistance Program, the Special Fund of the United Nations, and the World Bank. Its representatives and advisers are present in literally every important center in the developing countries. What reason can there, accordingly, be for not being aware of, concerned about, what it is doing? But of course UNESCO is only the educational arm of the United Nations system. I consider it our manifest duty toward the many religious and lay people we are sending to developing countries to achieve in concert with others whatever progress toward the conquest of ignorance and dire poverty is possible.

It is, of course, true that as yet social scientists have not succeeded in formulating a satisfactory theoretical approach to the problems of economic and social development, and that therefore it is still not possible to do more than experiment on the basis of such rule-of-thumb assumptions as can be made in the field. If I return for a moment to hybrid corn, it is for the sake of pointing out how great the resources of science now are. There are some who feel—and Father Hesburgh is one of them—that if these resources were fully utilized, the face of the earth could be changed within the century, virtually making mass poverty a thing of the past. While others are less optimistic, pointing to our own underprivileged population and to the need for a kind of war on the ills which now beset large groups of our urban and rural fellow citizens, there is general agreement that if we wish to do so vigorously enough, it will soon be unnecessary to go about the world with our guilty consciences on our sleeves, comparing our pampered selves with the multitudinous poor tumbling with each new day deeper into the pit of despair. Such despair is assuredly no soil in which virtue can long bloom. Nor do these poor any longer possess the resignation to accept their lot. They are creeping out of their hovels and singing their hymns.

Who can doubt that higher education—and in a special sense Catholic higher education—is called upon to make the problem of economic and social development, including population control, a matter of deep and lasting concern? Of course the university, which is the research institution proper, will not act for its sake alone. Its effort is designed to make possible a planned and well-conceived convergence—economic, educational, scientific—of the available forces. Thus one cannot establish a network of satisfactory primary schools without trained teachers, and these can come only from teacher-training colleges. And these, in turn, do not simply spring up out of the ground. Much precious time has been wasted in some parts of the world because of failure to realize soon enough that this cycle of educational activities cannot be circumvented.

Things would appear to be comparable in so far as the population problem is concerned. I do not think that anyone has a solution, but no less august a personage than Pope Paul VI has urged those among us who are competent to find one. Yes, it is possible to separate sexual indulgence from pregnancy by supplying steroids in sufficient quantities—that is, it is possible as long as the supply lasts, as is currently being found out in Puerto Rico. But the basic questions go far deeper. Why do people want children who must be reared in a misery even greater than that of the parents? Can religious and moral training inculcate the idea that loving and responsible parenthood must take precedence over the desire for biological reproduction? Is the practice of rhythm a practical possibility? Interestingly enough there are some who believe it might be easier to introduce the rhythm method into relatively primitive societies than it is to make it acceptable in even some comparatively Catholic countries which have attained to a high level of economic achievement.

I myself know nothing whatever about possible answers to any of these questions. But I believe I can say with some assurance that one could use the resources of American education to give the Catholic population, at least—not all at once but also not so slowly that it would require a century to bring it about—some genuine awareness of what economic and social development means to them in terms of understanding and of service. Clearly we have a solemn duty to bring this awareness about. We may argue as to whether a given Papal

Encyclical—*Pacem in terris,* for example—is a congeries of articles of faith. There can be no question, however, about the fact that no Christian can write off the New Testament; and this is literally quite frighteningly explicit about our individual and collective responsibility for the poor.

It seems to me that the point of focus here is the secondary school, in which social studies ought to include not only what is relatively easy and even pleasant, namely, some course work in what are termed non-Western or world cultures, but a quite explicit and searching concern with the problems of economic and social development. If there were no other reason for advancing this suggestion, it would suffice to point out that sending heroic men and women to developing countries is sheer waste, in every sense other than bearing witness to the faith of the Church, unless the tasks to which they are committed are understood. But there are other reasons in plenty. One of them obviously is that the graduates of Catholic secondary schools—or Catholic youngsters in other schools—will be gravely disadvantaged in discussion unless they are adequately prepared.

Why should not the Catholic Association for International Peace consider this task or project one which it could undertake with considerable benefit to us all? If on the basis of institutional memberships, of secondary schools, and as well of colleges, it could hammer out through consultation and discussion an appropriate course of study; if knowledgeable persons in this country or in others directly affected could be utilized as resource speakers; and if adequate bibliographies could be prepared—then, it seems to me at least, the Association could move into the main stream of education down which, after all, the cargo of the future will be carried. This meeting testifies to the clear insight and genuine zeal of those who organized it. Can we make it the beginning of a carefully discerned movement toward a goal?

Among the curious things about our era in history is that while larger numbers of people outside the Church see in it a potential source of strength for overcoming what has been and still is monstrous evil in the world, far too many products of Catholic education fail to see any relevance between religion and the world in which they live other than that which is perennially suggested by the inevitable mortality of the human race. Everybody knows that either we shall rise from the dead, as our Lord and Master did, or that our faith is in vain. There are very many, within the Church and outside it, who deeply and sincerely hope that this our central creed is justified. They like, even when they cannot quite believe, what we say about eternal life. But they do not think that we approach the problems of this world realistically. And in all frankness I would say that we do not. The next ten years will tell the story. I urge the Catholic Association for International Peace to do everything in its power to alter the situation.

600 Million Latin Americans
in the Year 2000?

Calvert L. Dedrick

In his foreign-aid message to Congress in March 1962 President Kennedy spoke of the "coming decade of development" which would look toward "the ultimate day when all nations can be self-reliant and when foreign aid will no longer be needed." Then he said:

> However, this will not be an easy task. The magnitude of the problem is staggering. In Latin America, for example, population growth is already threatening to outpace economic growth—and in some parts of the continent living standards are actually declining.
>
> In 1945 the population of our twenty sister American republics was 145 million. It is now greater than that of the United States and by the year 2000, less than forty years away, Latin-American population will be 592 million, compared with 312 million for the United States.
>
> Latin America will have to double its real income in the next thirty years simply to maintain already low standards of living.

The estimates of 592 million people in Latin America and 312 million in Northern America were taken directly from a United Nations study completed in 1958.[1] Nearly all the population censuses taken in Latin America in the period

[1] United Nations, *The Future Growth of World Population*, Population Studies No. 28. ("Medium" assumption used. The "low" assumption gave 445 million; and the "high" assumption, 651 million.)

1960–1964 indicate that these 1958 estimates were conservative. It is not unrealistic, therefore, to consider the possibility of 600 million people in Latin America by, or possibly even before, the year 2000. It would be preferable for all concerned to overestimate rather than underestimate the future population of Latin America.

Diversity of the Latin-American Region

Before considering what an addition of 394 million people would mean to the approximately 206 million in Latin America in 1960, let us note some facts about Latin America and its statistics. Latin America can be defined as the twenty republics of Central America, South America, and the Caribbean. This area is one of extremes both as to man and nature; highly cultured peoples who are at home in the elite circles of Europe and the United States, and indigenous peoples who have not substantially changed their ways since the Spanish and Portuguese first settled in their lands during the sixteenth century; workers with automated equipment producing electronic devices, and farmers who plant their crops with sticks and hoes; jet airplanes flying from modern airports in large cities over great expanses of mountains and forests dotted with farms and villages connected only by trails over which most products are carried by human beings. Not only is Latin America, as a region, an area of extreme contrasts and rapid transition, but so, too, are most of the twenty component countries. Demographically, however, there are numerous generalizations which apply to a large number of the individual countries as well as to Latin America as a region. Argentina and Uruguay are the most frequent and notable exceptions to demographic generalizations for this region because they have attained lower birth, death, and growth rates.

Availability of Latin-American Statistics

Statistics in general, and demographic statistics in particular, in Latin America are nearly as diverse in quantity and quality as are the countries themselves. The first relatively complete population census of this region was taken during the period 1947 to 1953. Only Peru and Uruguay failed to get a total population count and a classification by age, sex, education, occupation, and other characteristics. For the period 1960–1964 only Bolivia and Haiti have not taken population censuses, although most countries have not yet published detailed reports.

Annual birth and death data are reliable for only a very few countries, thus limiting greatly the possibility of intercensal estimates and trend analyses. Because of this, it is advisable to speak of a probable range of values for demographic variables rather than place too much reliance on reported rates, especially of births and deaths, or calculated values such as life expectancy.

With these warnings in mind as to the diversity of Latin America and its statistics, let us examine: (1) whether it is at all reasonable to assume that this region might increase from about 206 million people in 1960 to 600 million in the year 2000; (2) what characteristics this rapid increase will give the population of this area; and (3) the probable effect of these characteristics on economic and social development.

Rapidity of Population Increase

In these days of billion-dollar expenditures to reach the moon and of megatons of atomic bombs, many people are unimpressed by a figure of "only" 400 million people, or a population increase of "only" 3 per cent per year. Stated in other terms, the 400 million people is nearly the total population of the world in 1650, when the Pilgrims and other colonists were first settling the eastern United States. It is one-sixth of the increase in world's population during the three hundred years from 1650 to 1950. It is more than 2¼ times the total population of the United States and Canada in 1950.

It has become common knowledge that "Latin America has the most rapidly increasing population in the world." But this, too, seems to have little real meaning to the average person until he studies estimates of the world's population and our own. For example, as a proportion of the world's population, Latin America has increased from 2.7 per cent in 1900 to 4.9 per cent in 1920, and 6.9 per cent in 1960. If the United Nations estimates are right, the proportion will be 9.5 per cent in the year 2000, despite the high increases expected in other parts of the world such as China, South Asia, and Africa.

It can be pointed out, with good reason, that past population projections for the United States and Europe have been quite inaccurate. The question then becomes: Are these Latin-American projections for thirty-five years into the future really reasonable? To answer this it is necessary to examine the available statistics on births and deaths, and consider the social and economic factors which affect fertility and mortality. Migration into and out of this area can be disregarded for present purposes. Also omitted from the following discussion is the important subject of the food supply. Although some experts question the probability of changing the traditional, relatively inefficient agricultural practices of Latin-American farmers fast enough to keep up with this projected population increase, there seems to be little question that the region as a whole (but certainly not all countries, e.g., El Salvador and Haiti) has sufficient undeveloped, arable land to feed 600 million people *if modern agricultural practices were used.*

The Declining Death Rate

An increasingly rapid decline in the death rate has been an outstanding demographic characteristic of Latin America during the past sixty years. And this trend can be expected to continue during the balance of this century in those countries which still have high mortality rates. Again we should note the great diversity of this area both as between countries and within countries. As in all parts of the world, medical advances come first to large cities, then smaller cities and towns, and most slowly to villages and the rural population. Unfortunately, mortality statistics for most countries do not permit a detailed, year-to-year study of areas with specific social and economic characteristics; and for only a few countries are there reliable data to show mortality trends for as much as forty years.

Illustrative, but not necessarily typical, of the rapid downward trend of mortality in Latin America are the following registered crude death rates for selected countries:

REGISTERED CRUDE DEATHS PER 1,000
POPULATION PER YEAR [2]

Area	1921–1925	1955–1958	Per cent decrease
Argentina	14.4	8.4	42
Chile	30.3	12.5	59
El Salvador	23.9	13.5	44
Mexico	25.5	12.9	49
Venezuela	19.1	9.9	48

The Economic Commission for Latin America has published estimated crude death rates for all Latin-American countries for two five-year periods, 1945 to 1950 and 1955 to 1960. A significant lowering of the death rate is shown during this decade for every country of the area. These data attest to the success of campaigns for pure drinking water, immunization against communicable diseases, school hygiene programs, maternal and child clinics, improved medical care for workers and their families covered by social-security systems, etc. Especially significant is the rapid reduction of infant mortality which is reflected in an increasing survivorship of the newborn. These are principally governmental programs which require little individual knowledge or motivation.

Although these governmental health programs operate most effectively in the larger urban centers, many of them are being extended quite rapidly to smaller places and even the rural population. An as yet unstudied force for mortality reduction is the word-of-mouth communication of health practices from the often-illiterate migrant to the city to his family in remote rural areas.

[2] From *Population Bulletin of the United Nations*, No. 6, 1962, Table III.10, p. 32

In those countries where the mortality rate was highest the decrease has been most pronounced, but in all countries, without exception, mortality has been reduced considerably. In keeping with this, all projections of population prepared for the region have automatically implied the assumption of a declining crude death rate or, more precisely, a continued rise in expectation of life at birth.[3]

Life tables which provide a measure of "expectation of life at birth" as well as survivorship factors which picture the age and sex structure of the population have been calculated for relatively few countries and cities of Latin America because of the unreliability of data on vital statistics and corrections which are required in published census data. However, the United Nations has assembled some significant figures on life expectancy at birth from which the following table has been extracted:

[3] Carmen A. Miro, "The Population of Latin America," *Demography*, Population Association of America, 1964.

GAIN IN EXPECTATION OF LIFE AT BIRTH
FOR SELECTED AREAS OF LATIN AMERICA [4]

Country or area	Period	Expectation of life at birth (years) [a]	Average annual gain since preceding period (years)
Chile	1930	40.7	—
	1940	42.0	0.13
	1952	51.9	0.82
Costa Rica	1949–1951	55.9	—
	1955–1957	62.0	1.00
Mexico	1930	33.3	—
	1940	38.9	0.56
	1949–1951	49.7	1.08
Brazil—Federal District	1939–1941	42.5	—
	1949–1951	52.9	1.04
Peru—Lima City	1933–1935	39.0	—
	1940–1943	46.1	0.95

[a] Both sexes.

The annual increase in expected longevity at birth was more than one year for each calendar year of elapsed time for all of Mexico (1940 to 1949–1951) and the Federal District (Rio de Janeiro) of Brazil (1939–1941 to 1949–1951). The longevity of the Chilean population, which increased only 1.3 years in the decade 1930 to 1940, went up more than six times as fast between 1940 and 1952. We await with interest the life tables which will be calculated for the period 1959 to 1961. It is highly probable that they will reveal a continued drop in mortality and increase of longevity in Latin America.

[4] *Population Bulletin of the United Nations*, No. 6, 1962, Table III.13, p. 35.

Relatively Constant Birth Rates

Births, rather than deaths, are most influential in determining the age structure of a population, as we note later. The fact that birth rates in Latin America and many other areas of the world are more resistant to downward pressures than are death rates is general knowledge. But few people realize how much of a time lag really occurs in the adjustment of the childbearing behavior of a culture to more favorable conditions of low mortality; nor are the factors which influence fertility as well understood as those which determine mortality.

Birth statistics, too, are inadequate for most of Latin America. Traditionally, in Spanish and Portuguese areas, registration of births is under the Civil Registry organization of the Ministry of Interior (Home Affairs), and is not, nor can it be, rigidly enforced. In most countries birth certificates are not required for school entry and other purposes, and they are often hard to get. Also, the legal purpose of the Civil Registry, originally to establish paternity for property inheritance and other purposes, can be satisfied by the registration of a birth years after it occurs. For these and other reasons only in recent times and in selected countries are there reliable birth statistics.

The most recent estimates by the Economic Commission for Latin America are presented in Table 5, at the end of this paper, for two periods, 1945 to 1950, and 1955 to 1960.

Unlike the corresponding table for deaths, there is no substantial decrease in the crude birth rate during this decade for any of the countries except Cuba, Argentina, and Uruguay. The table indicates the relative inexactness of the data by providing a range (two figures) for each country. If, arbitrarily, a tabulation is made of the mid-points of these ranges, the following table results for 1955–1960:

Crude birth rate per 1,000 population	Number of countries
48 and over	8
44.0 to 47.9	6
40.0 to 43.9	2
36.0 to 39.9	1
Less than 36.0	3

These are almost unbelievably high birth rates even considering the youthful average age of the population of these countries.

Following is a tabulation of the "gross reproduction rate," a more refined measure of the fertility of these countries, estimated by the United Nations. The data are not entirely comparable because of differences in their time reference as shown in Table 5.

ESTIMATED GROSS REPRODUCTION
RATE OF LATIN AMERICA [5]

Gross reproduction rate	Number of countries
3.5 to 3.9	2
3.0 to 3.4	9
2.5 to 2.9	5
2.0 to 2.4	2
1.5 to 1.9	—
1.0 to 1.4	2 [a]

[a] Argentina and Uruguay

Some Cultural Factors Affecting Fertility

Is this high fertility of Latin-American countries likely to
continue for a generation or more? Or may it drop rapidly in
the near future to the levels now characteristic of the more
industrialized countries? Although no demographer is apt to
give a dogmatic answer to these questions, there is a general
consensus that the decline in fertility in Latin America will be
quite slow unless there is a substantial change in the cultural
values and characteristics which affect parenthood. The following are some of these cultural values and characteristics:

(1) The "large family pattern" has existed throughout the
history of this area, especially among rural and village people.
To have many offspring is one of the proofs that a man is
"muy macho" and that his wife is a good wife and mother. For

[5] The gross reproduction rate level is an estimate of the number of
daughters that the average woman would bear in a group of women
who started life at the same time, if all members of this group survived
to the end of the childbearing ages and if they were subject to the age-
specific birth rates prevailing during a given year, or years. One may
double this rate to obtain a rough approximation of the total number
of children, including sons, the average woman would bear.

hundreds of years high infant and maternal mortality has been a factor thwarting the attainment of large families.

(2) Early marriage of girls, except those in the upper social class (who appear most often in Spanish literature), is accepted as natural. Census tables of number of children ever born by age of mother show significant numbers of children born to mothers as young as thirteen to fifteen years of age, especially in rural areas.

(3) Common-law marriages—in Spanish called "consensual unions"—are culturally acceptable in many areas. Formal marriage is still considered an upper-class behavior in many rural areas and among the poorer class of urban areas. In 1950 the censuses of seven countries showed 20 per cent or more of the population over fifteen years of age as living in consensual unions. Although many of these unions are relatively stable, some lasting for the lifetime of the couple, others are of shorter duration.

(4) Employment of children at an early age, not only in agricultural but nonagricultural activities, is not frowned on by the community if it is a large and/or poor family. This results in the sacrifice of the education of many children and swells the supply of unskilled labor.

(5) Ignorance of an elementary knowledge of human physiology and hygiene has resulted from generations of illiterate ancestors and the taboo on the discussion of sex and procreation.

It should be remembered that the mothers of most of the children who will be born during the next thirty-five years are already living and have acquired these and the other cultural characteristics and values of their community.

Cultural characteristics and values such as those must all be changed if the fertility of Latin America is to decrease. This is a much slower process, more personal and far less subject to governmental programs than the reduction of mortality. Given these facts, it is unlikely that there will be a *rapid* decline in the birth rate of Latin America as a whole within the next generation.

Some decrease in fertility is almost certain to occur, however, because of such trends as urbanization, industrialization, increased educational level, rising standard of living, increasing proportion of the middle class, and occupational opportunities for women, etc. An analysis of census statistics and of the results of special studies which have been conducted in this area shows that all of these trends are associated with lower birth rates in Latin America as they are in more industrialized countries. But much more research is needed on factors affecting fertility in Latin America than appears to be attainable in the near future. There are relatively few indigenous programs for research of this type; such research is still frowned on by many governmental leaders, by the Communist party line, and by the Catholic Church; and the personnel to conduct such research is very limited.

To return now to a question raised earlier: Is it reasonable to assume and to plan for at least the next five years that Latin America will have a total population of 600 million by the year 2000?

Results of the 1960 cycle of censuses supported by more reliable measures of population growth (e.g., vital statistics and school population estimates), indicate that the population of Latin America will reach 315 million by 1965.[6] This esti-

[6] United Nations/ECLA, Statistical Bulletin for Latin America, Vol. I, No. 1, March 1964, Table 3.

mate was prepared by the U. N. Demographic Research and
Training Center in Santiago, Chile, and published by the
Economic Commission for Latin America.

ECLA estimates also show that the probable population
increase for this area during the five years 1960 to 1965 will be
(one can almost say "has been") in the order of 31 million
people. This is almost exactly the sum of the 1960 population
of the twelve smallest countries (in population) of Latin
America.[7] Or, to translate this 1960 to 1965 increase to an
annual amount and United States areas, the 6 million-plus
Latin-American increase *per year* is the equivalent of adding
the population (1960) of the state of New Jersey, or the three
states of Massachusetts, New Hampshire, and Vermont.

The Age Structure of Latin America

A sustained high birth rate results in a "young" population,
with a large proportion in the early ages—preschool, school,
and young adults. Rapidly declining death rates, especially
when the drop in infant mortality is a major factor in the
decline, has the same effect on the age structure. From a
long-time point of view, the birth rate has more effect on the
age structure of a population than the death rate. Combine
these two trends—high fertility and decreasing mortality—
and the result is the unusually young population of Latin
America.

The United Nations has recently published a study that
assembles and analyzes the recent economic and demographic
data and presents a cautious analysis of the interrelation

[7] Bolivia, Costa Rica, Dominican Republic, Ecuador, El Salvador,
Guatemala, Haiti, Honduras, Nicaragua, Panama, Paraguay, and
Uruguay.

between these two fields.[8] The United Nations report states that the unusually young age structure of Latin America has a bearing on many aspects of economic development. The following quotations and abstracts from the above-mentioned report highlight this fact:

The large proportion of child population is another of the characteristic demographic features of Latin America. It is mainly attributable to the high birth rates prevalent in the region and in lesser measure to the drop in mortality, particularly among the lower age groups. Over 40 per cent of the population of Latin America is under fifteen years of age. The corresponding proportion fluctuates around 30 per cent in countries like Canada and the United States, and is still smaller in most of the European countries. Again, the percentage of old people is lower in Latin America than in other regions. Thus, while in Europe, North America, and Oceania it amounts to approximately 10 per cent of the total population, in Latin America the number of persons of sixty-five years of age or over barely exceeds 3 per cent of the total population of the region. If the potentially active population (fifteen to sixty-four years) is considered, it works out at 55 per cent of the total in Latin America, as against 60 and even 65 per cent in the more advanced countries. This means that while the potentially active population has to bear the brunt of the maintenance, education, and medical care of 45 per cent of the total population of Latin America, in those countries of Europe and America where income levels are higher it only has to provide in these respects for 35 or at the most 40 per cent of its younger or older compatriots. This population characteristic of Latin America is ultimately reflected in a much more burdensome economic effort on the part of countries which, in addition, are at a less advanced stage of development.

Because of the high proportion of school-age population, the labor force (economically active population) averages

[8] United Nations. *The Economic Development of Latin America in the Post-War Period*, New York, 1964.

only slightly more than one-third of the total population, whereas in other areas with a different age structure the labor force comprises 40 or more per cent of the total. The average productivity of the labor force is less than in other areas because of such factors as the youth and lack of education of the active population. For example, the United Nations report states:

Another constant in the Latin-American countries (and in underdeveloped countries in general) is the early age at which both the male and female population enter gainful employment, under the pressure of the need to swell the meager family income. This affects the level of education of the labor force by preventing the attainment of higher standards of general education or technical training. It was estimated, around 1950, that out of approximately 100 million persons in Latin America aged fifteen years or over, no fewer than 40 million were illiterate; and it is likely that since then this number has increased, although the proportion of the total may have been reduced. In relation to the degree of urbanization and industrialization attained by the region, the percentage of illiterate persons is high in comparison with the figures for other parts of the world, even including some where per-capita income levels are lower.

As regards the structure of employment and the level of education in general, attention has already been drawn to the correlation existing between the percentage of illiteracy and the proportion of the labor force employed in agricultural activities.

This brief survey does not permit the inclusion of data on the enormous problems that this age structure of the population imposes on the already inadequate educational facilities of most of the countries of Latin America. In the United States we have been concerned during the past decade with the problems of educating our postwar "baby boom." In Latin America not only is there a much greater "baby boom," but certain areas report that one-third or more of the children who should be beginning their studies in the first grade are unable to do so because of absence or inaccessibility of schools, teachers, books, and, sometimes, the lack of sufficient community interest to make the sacrifices necessary to provide educational facilities. For many countries of this area the problem is not "How much do we need for education?" Rather, it is "How much can we afford to put into education in view of the requirement for expenditures which will promote more rapid economic growth?" A basic policy debate is in process in some countries as to whether, given very limited funds for education, this sum should be spent on better education (higher quality and more years) for those already attending school, or in attaining, as rapidly as possible, some education for everyone to wipe out illiteracy.

Let us now depart from a consideration of the quantitative aspects of population growth in Latin America and consider some of the important sociological trends which arise in part from the cultural background and historical trends in this area.

Latin America has been an area of political ferment since earliest colonial times. Through hundreds of years it has been the land of the "haves" and the "have nots"—largely a two-class society. During the Spanish regime, and even now from the point of view of the large landholders, an increasing and docile (preferably illiterate) labor supply was advantageous for the agricultural economy and the easy maintenance of peace and order.

This resulted in a policy of selective education and a limitation of personal mobility both as to space and status. With relative suddenness, as defined by historical trends, the countries of this area have emerged from colonial cultures and characteristics to try to catch up with the more industrialized and democratic governments of the world. Inevitably, however, there remain cultural characteristics and values, especially in the rural areas, which are quite different from those which have been developed during the long road to industrialization in the more economically advanced countries of the world. We have noted above some of the cultural characteristics and values which directly affect fertility. Let us now consider some which interact with the relative youthfulness of the population and affect economic and social development.

1.   Traditionally, education beyond the primary-school level placed one in a favored social class, and permitted an escape from manual labor to white-collar employment in business or the government. Modernization of the economy, however, will require more education even to perform many non-white-collar jobs.

2. An economy and population which grew slowly was able to absorb its population increase. It mattered little what level of education or skill he had acquired, a new worker could find a job. The present-day youths who are entering the labor market, especially those with only limited schooling, find it necessary to have "connections" to land a job in business or industry as well as (traditionally) government.

3.   Girls required much less education than boys because there were relatively few socially approved economic opportunities outside of the family farm or business. But modern girls are becoming educated, entering the labor market in competition with boys, and sometimes perform more efficiently, partly, at least, because they seem not so preoccupied with outside activities such as politics and sports.

4.   Universities and secondary schools in Latin America

have been the traditional training grounds for political activity in addition to imparting nonpolitical knowledge. The autonomy of most universities often saved these institutions from complete dictator domination and kept alive a government opposition. The curriculum was often designed for the sons of the rich and middle class who were destined to go into law, medicine, or military service, or to manage the family fortune. Until relatively recently, few university graduates planned to become skilled technicians and managers for industry. The great dream of many of the graduates was to get into politics.

5. Traditionally, the younger generation expected to live in a better but not too different world than their parents, regardless of their level in society. Today, because of the very rapid demographic and economic changes, increasing literacy, daily communication with the outside world through newspapers, radio, and television, the youth are living in a world which is not fully understood by their grandparents or even their parents. Just as the United States-born children of immigrants were, to their parents, shockingly "different" and their attitude and behavior were often incomprehensible, so, too, there is a cultural gap between generations in Latin America.

These sociological factors and many others which are difficult if not impossible to measure have a direct bearing on the interrelation between demographic and economic trends in Latin America. They also greatly affect political stability without which economic development becomes almost impossible. Here again is an urgent need for demographic, sociological, and other research which is not being met in Latin America.

The results of the demographic trends which we have noted, occurring within present-day economic conditions and the cultural characteristics and values of "old" Latin America, provide an almost ideal setting for the growth of communist ideas and ideals. The literate young, from those barely able to read and write to the university students, feel frustrated to meet their personal needs and aspirations for the future. They realize that there must be a change, and want to be a part of the "new look" in economics and politics. They want their government to do something to help them realize their aspirations: to get an education; to hold a secure job, unaffected by political change; to have a comfortable home; to marry young and have a large family; in short, to have an abundant life. They are impressed by glowing propaganda which shows the tremendous advances from underdevelopment to development which have occurred not only in the U. S. S. R. and China but in the smaller Communist countries. They are also impressed by accounts of the high standards of living in the U. S. A. and other more industrialized countries which produce so many of the goods they want.

All of these factors tend to direct attention to economic and political systems rather than to such fundamentals as people, resources, and public administration. Least of all, I fear, does the average young man in Latin America realize that the slow progress being made in economic and social development is, to a large degree, the result of the demographic trends and characteristics of his people. Nor does he realize that the slow progress being made in economic and social development is, in a major way, related to the fact that he is *"muy macho"* and wants his wife to prove it by having many children.

TABLE 1
ESTIMATED WORLD POPULATION AND
RATE OF INCREASE BY REGIONS

Area	Population 1960 (millions)	Rate of increase 1950–1960 (per cent)
World	2,995	1.8
America	414	2.1
North America	199	1.8
Latin America	215	2.8
Asia	1,679	1.9
Europe	427	0.8
Oceania	16.5	2.4
Soviet Union	214.4	1.7

Source: United Nations, *The Economic Development of Latin America*, New York, 1964. Tables 78 and 82.

TABLE 2
PROJECTED POPULATION OF THE WORLD,
BY MAJOR REGIONS: 1950, 1975, AND 2000
(Medium assumption)

	Projected population Millions			Per cent increase	
	1950	1975	2000	1950–1975	1975–2000
World total	2,497	3,828	6,267	53	64
Northern America	168	240	312	43	30
Latin America	163	303	592	86	95
Asia (excl. USSR)	1,380	2,210	3,870	60	75
Europe (incl. USSR)	574	751	947	31	26
Africa	199	303	517	52	71
Oceania	13	21	29	59	40

Source: United Nations, *The Future Growth of World Population*, Population Studies No. 28, New York, 1958. Tables 5 and 6, for population estimates and projections.

TABLE 3
ESTIMATES OF THE TOTAL POPULATION OF
LATIN AMERICA: 1650 TO 2000
(Millions)

Year	Twenty Latin-American Republics	Central and South America, and Caribbean Islands	
	ECLA [a]	U.N. [b]	Willcox [b]
1650	—	—	−7
1750	—	—	10
1800	—	—	23
1850	—	—	33
1900	—	—	63
1920	—	92	
1925	92.9	—	
1930	102.6	110	
1935	112.7	—	
1940	124.1	132	
1945	137.9	—	
1950	156.1	163	
1955	178.9	—	
1960	205.9	—	
1965	237.0	—	
1970	273.1	—	
1975	315.0	303	
1980	363.6	—	
2000	—	592	

Sources:

[a] United Nations/ECLA, *Statistical Bulletin for Latin America*, Vol. I, No. 1, 1964, Table 3.

[b] United Nations, *Determinants and Consequences of Population Trends*, New York, 1953, Table 2, for estimates prior to 1950. United Nations, *The Future Growth of World Population*, Population Studies No. 28, for 1950 estimate, and for projections to 1975 and 2000 (medium assumption).

TABLE 4
ESTIMATED CRUDE DEATH RATE AND EXPECTATION OF LIFE AT BIRTH OF LATIN AMERICA, BY COUNTRIES: 1945–50 AND 1955–60
(Unofficial estimates)

Area or country	Crude death rate per 1,000 population		Expectation of life at birth (years)	
	1945–1950	1955–1960	1945–1950	1955–1960
LATIN AMERICA	*17–19*	*13–15*	*45–49*	*52–56*
SOUTH AMERICA	16–19	12–15	45–50	52–56
Argentina	9–10	8– 9	61–62	64–66
Bolivia	23–27	20–25	36–42	40–45
Brazil	17–23	11–16	40–48	50–58
Colombia	17–21	14–17	44–48	48–53
Chile	17–19	12–13	47–51	53–56
Ecuador	20–25	15–20	38–43	43–48
Paraguay	15–20	12–16	48–52	50–58
Peru	18–24	13–18	40–48	48–55
Uruguay	8– 9	7– 9	62–65	65–68
Venezuela	16–20	10–15	45–50	53–57
CENTRAL AMERICA AND CARIBBEAN	17–21	14–17	44–48	50–54
Costa Rica	12–16	9–13	52–58	56–62
Cuba	11–15	9–13	52–58	56–62
Dominican Republic	20–25	16–20	38–45	44–50
El Salvador	18–23	14–18	40–47	48–52
Guatemala	22–27	20–24	37–42	40–46
Haiti	25–30	20–28	32–38	36–45
Honduras	18–24	15–20	40–46	45–50
Mexico	17–20	13–16	45–48	51–55
Nicaragua	16–20	12–17	45–52	50–55
Panama	14–17	9–13	48–53	54–59

Source: United Nations Economic Commission for Latin America, *Boletín Económico de América Latina*, Vol. VII, No. 1, Santiago de Chile, October 1962. Table 4.

TABLE 5
ESTIMATED CRUDE BIRTH RATES AND GROSS REPRODUCTION RATES (for selected years) OF LATIN AMERICA, BY COUNTRIES: 1945–1950 and 1955–1960
(Unofficial estimates)

Area or country	Births per 1,000 population		Gross reproduction rate	
	1945–1950	1955–1960	Date	Level
LATIN AMERICA	41–43	41–43		
SOUTH AMERICA	40–42	40–42		
Argentina	25–26	23–24	1961	1.4
Bolivia	41–45	41–45	1940–1945	2.9
Brazil	43–47	43–47	1940–1945	3.0
Chile	34–37	35–38	1960	2.4
Colombia	44–47	43–46	1941–1946	2.9
Ecuador	45–50	45–50	1940–1945	3.2
Paraguay	45–50	45–50	1940–1945	2.9
Peru	42–48	42–48	1930–1935	3.1
Uruguay	20–23	19–22	1957	1.3
Venezuela	44–48	45–50	1960	3.1
CENTRAL AMERICA AND CARIBBEAN	43–47	43–47		
Costa Rica	44–48	45–50	1960	3.5
Cuba	32–36	30–34	1943–1948	2.1
Dominican Republic	48–54	48–54	1950–1955	3.2
El Salvador	44–48	44–48	1961	3.3
Guatemala	48–52	48–52	1960	3.4
Haiti	42–50	42–50	1935–1940	2.8
Honduras	45–50	45–50	1951–1956	3.6
Mexico	44–48	44–47	1960	3.1
Nicaragua	45–52	45–52	1940–1945	3.1
Panama	38–42	39–42	1960	2.7

Source: For birth rate, United Nations Economic Commission for Latin America, *Boletín Económico de América Latina*, Vol. VII, No. 1, Santiago de Chile, October 1962. Table 4. For gross reproduction rate, Carmen A. Miró, "The Population of Latin America," *Demography*, Vol. I, No. 1, The Population Association of America, Chicago, 1964.

TABLE 6

TOTAL POPULATION AND PER CENT OF THE POPULATION
OF THE UNITED STATES AND OF MEXICO IN EACH
AGE GROUP: 1960

Age group (years)	Total population (thousands)		Per cent in age group		Cumulative percentage	
	U.S.A.	Mexico	U.S.A.	Mexico	U.S.A.	Mexico
All Ages	178,467	34,923	100.0	100.0 ª	100.0	100.0 ª
0–4	20,207	5,777	11.3	16.6	11.3	16.6
5–9	18,559	5,317	10.4	15.3	21.7	31.9
10–14	16,733	4,358	9.4	12.6	31.1	44.5
15–19	13,215	3,535	7.4	10.3	38.5	54.8
20–24	10,729	2,947	6.0	8.5	44.5	63.3
25–29	10,805	2,505	6.1	7.1	50.6	70.4
30–34	11,884	2,052	6.7	5.8	57.2	76.2
35–39	12,442	1,921	7.0	5.5	64.2	81.7
40–44	11,513	1,361	6.5	3.9	70.6	85.6
45–49	10,885	1,234	6.1	3.5	76.7	89.1
50–54	9,662	1,063	5.4	3.0	82.1	92.1
55–59	8,567	800	4.8	2.2	86.9	94.3
60–64	7,093	745	4.0	2.1	90.9	96.4
65+	16,173	1,195	9.1	3.6	100.0	100.0
Unknown	—	114		ª		ª

ª Per cent calculation excludes unknown ages.

Demographic Instability:
Resolution or Retrogression in Asia

Irene B. Taeuber

The population dynamics of the developing Asian countries are transitional or unstable. These words are used advisedly. Reduced death rates, high birth rates, high rates of population growth—these cannot continue indefinitely or even for substantial periods of time. The question is not change but the nature of the change and the conditions under which it occurs.

There may be resolution through declining birth rates; there may be the retrogression of increasing death rates. There need be no one process of change, for there is no demography that is specifically Asian. There is no Asian rate of growth in a continent that includes Japan, Siberia, China, India, and Israel; no Asian birth rate in a continent that includes the Ryukyus, Taiwan, Java, and East Pakistan; no Asian death rate in a continent that includes Hong Kong, Ceylon, Tibet, and Saudi Arabia.

Some containment of the diversities is essential if an argument is to be meaningful and if we are to remain reasonably consistent with the assigned topic of "Asia." Hereafter, then, we shall use the word "Asia" to refer to that area below the USSR and east of Iran; this is the region of activities of the United Nations Economic Commission for Asia and the Far East, commonly known as ECAFE. Japan, Soviet Asia, and

60

the demographically modernizing Chinese populations on China's perimeter will be considered specifically in various contexts, as will other regional groupings of the geographic continent.

The fact that continents or other geographic regions are not the critical divisive units in today's world leads to continuing inconsistencies between the topic of Asia and the demographic argument, for that argument is not geographically specific. The essential task, however, is an analytic approach to the interrelations of population pressures, population growth, and the maintenance of the peace. The eventual question is whether there are or are not general relations between population and peace.

A logically structured approach to the problem would be feasible, but there is a nagging question as to the definition of the logical. There are theoretical possibilities, but there are also human realities, the prevalent concepts of those realities, and an ongoing demographic dynamism whose alternate paths are influenced by governmental decisions and individual choices.

The initial approach is a limited empirical one; it involves the question of the future of the populations of the countries and the regions. Given the prospective size, characteristics, and rates of growth of populations, it is possible to construct alternate series of hypotheses as to the economic, social, and therefore political implications. If the argument is extended to include the preservation of the peace, it has to include the assumption, whether implicit or explicit, that population increase beyond a specific though perhaps mobile point connotes misery, internal insurrection, international interference, and hence the dissolution of the peace.

The Forces of the Future

The projection of populations into the future is simple or
complex, depending on the analytical techniques and com-
puter facilities. The estimation of future populations is a
different problem, for sophistication in measurement and skill
in computation do not necessarily yield probability estimates
of the future course of growth or the components of growth.
Sad experience in past projections has convinced students of
Asia that the continuities of the past need not persist in the
future. Stage transition models and concepts of an Asian
recapitulation of a European past repose today in the archives
of demography. The record of projections across the great
divide from colonial to national states is also sad, for this was a
projection from archaic to modernizing conditions affecting
mortality in a setting in which fertility remained relatively
unchanging. Anticipations of transitions in fertility with in-
dependence have not yet been realized, perhaps because transitions are products of associated economic and social changes
rather than responses to the contained pressures of the gap
between births and deaths.

The estimation of the future is not yet possible as other
than a hypothetical construct. There have been major lags in
public recognition of the complexities in solutions to problems involving high birth rates. There are prevalent beliefs
that discussions of explosions, knowledge of birth control,
policies by governments, or unleashings of external assistance
will produce quick responses among peoples, sharp declines in
birth rates, and therefore swiftly slowing rates of growth.

These anticipations and aspirations that prevail so widely
today ignore the lethargies of great societies and the time

required for biological transformations in populations whose life spans are those of man. Perhaps, though, those who label hopes of quick transformations unsophisticated are themselves naïve. The phenomenon of population growth as it is occurring in the Asian context is new in world history. The responses of governments and peoples to that growth are therefore unknown. They may also be quite distinctive in contrast with past experience.

The seemingly simple task of estimating the future of Asian populations thus involves the assessment of uncharted courses. That study of the past which would be significant is scarcely touched; much of that study of the present which would be relevant is not yet structured in analytic terms.

Responsibilities with reference to present and future, however, cannot be evaded by bewailing the absent research, for no analysis of the past of the developing countries would provide other than clues as to the future. The major determinants of the future lie in the responses of peoples in situations that are novel, not alone in Asian countries but in Latin America and in Africa. Seven of the forces and developments relevant to the determination of the demographic future may be listed:

1. Countries are now independent. Governments and people are dissatisfied with low economic levels and slow advance.

2. National, regional, and international organizations are concentrating on economic development and social change. In so far as developments are successful, there will be increasing levels of real income, improving nutrition, positive health and vitality, educational and other opportunities for children, occupational and social mobility for youth, and some

of the amenities that lie outside the areas of poverty, backwardness, and deprivation. In so far as developments fail, there are frustrations.

3. Knowledge of the associations of population growth and developmental achievement is widespread. There are some plans for national services in the family planning field, and there are some operating facilities for the achievement of knowledgeable populations with access to means.

4. There is no basis in administrative experience to guide the organization of effective programs in the broad field of birth control. The reasons are many: Inattention if not taboos that retard discussion, opinion formation, and the evolution of motivations; the delayed development of technologies in fields relevant to the induction of social change at village and family levels; the barriers to international assistance in fertility control except with circumlocution and indirection; the prevalent allocation of the field as one for crusade, conversion, and propaganda rather than as a proper field for appropriate concern in the core of government planning and developmental activity.

5. Scientific and technological advances, effective internal administration, and international assistance permit declines in death rates without immediate reference to economic and social development.

6. Scientific and technological work relevant to fertility control was long postponed; it is now in process and productive. There are currently available some means of contraception acceptable to and effective in some village settings. It is probable that more acceptable and more effective means will become available as scientific and technological work continues.

7. Population growth places pressures on families, villages,

and the institutions and administrative units of the larger society. There is therefore a possibility of swift changes in assessments, attitudes, and motivations with reference to operational decisions to plan family size.

Projections of the Future[1]

What, then, is the future? Here we have conjecture, computation, and speculation for the developing countries. Let us assume, with the United Nations staff, that mortality continues to decline, and that fertility is reduced by half within a thirty-year period after sustained decline begins. It is reasonable to assume, also, that the date of the beginning of decline is related to economic status and education, cultural receptivity, and the state of government policies and programs in population control.

If birth rates in the countries of Asia should be cut in half in the years between 1965 and 2000, the population that was 1.7 billion in 1960 would be 3.4 billion in 2000. Given continuously and fairly rapidly declining fertility, the population of the continent still doubles in the next thirty-five years! The rate of growth, estimated at 21 per cent for the decade from 1960 to 1970, declines to 17 per cent for the last decade in the century.

Despite the magnitude of the continuing growth, that

[1] The present and projected populations used in this study are those of the United Nations, issued in provisional form. United Nations Department of Economic and Social Affairs, *Provisional report on world population prospects as assessed in 1963.* ST/SOA/Ser.R/7. New York, 1964, iv, 316 pp. The final report with definitive figures will be published in the series, *Population Studies* (ST/SOA/Series A). This note also relies heavily on the United Nations' analyses of the future trends of mortality and fertility as presented in the *Population Bulletin of the United Nations*, No. 6, for mortality (Sales No: 62. XIII. 2), and No. 7 for fertility.

decline in fertility which was occurring would have significant and increasing relations to the dynamics of economic and social processes. Reduced rates of population growth facilitate economic growth; fewer children reduce burdens on families. Lesser rates of increase in school-age populations permit larger portions of educational expenditures to be devoted to qualitative improvements and extensions to more advanced levels rather than to numerical expansions whose achievement is the maintenance of present facilities for larger numbers.

Eventually, less rapidly increasing cohorts of youth entering the labor force ease the pressures for job expansion and lessen the hazards of underemployment and unemployment. Adequately trained and appropriately utilized youth contribute more to the productivity of the economy. Age structures less heavily weighted with youth facilitate savings and the utilization of savings in productive activities rather than the diversion of limited savings to the maintenance costs of increasing numbers. The dynamic interrelations of demographic and other factors facilitate further directional movement toward final resolution of the problems of population growth.

If the populations of the Asian countries are to increase from 1.7 billion in 1960 to 3.4 billion in 2000, under conditions of declining mortality and declining fertility, there must be rapid economic and social development. Such rapid economic development is essential if the increasing numbers of the people are to be fed, clothed, and housed; it they are not fed, they will not be alive to constitute the projected population for the future. The rapid social development is essential to the generation of the forces involved in the continuing decline of birth rates. Thus, economic and social development and declining birth rates are necessarily related if they are to be aspects of the Asian future. If they are, in fact, so related in the near and continuing future, Asian countries may begin the twenty-first century in a setting in which numbers are less pre-eminent among the many problems of development.

There is no necessary demographic doom throughout Asia; there are no inevitable demographic solutions to problems of economic growth and human advance in Asia. Yet it is no longer possible to avoid the evidence that there may be demographic doom in some sectors of Asia, as in some sectors elsewhere in the world. It is now possible, though, to point to such Asian countries as Japan, where there is solution, to such Asian countries as Taiwan, where economic and demographic advance are proceeding together.

The Implications of Continuity

The preceding discussion was based on the assumption that birth rates are reduced to half their present levels in most of the countries while death rates continue to decline. This, as we have noted, implies not alone rapid economic development but swift social change. What will be the population forecast if death rates continue downward while birth rates remain unchanged?

The implications of continuity in trends in world population may serve as preface to the consideration of the Asian regions. The population of this earth was estimated at 2.5 billion in 1950, 3.0 billion in 1960. If trends should continue to the year 2000, the population would be 7.5 billion. The increase of the half century from 1950 to 2000 would be 5 billion.[2] This would be sufficient to populate two additional

[2] The major problem with reference to the future projection involves the population of Mainland China; the major question with reference to the future population of Mainland China, given assump-

earths as this one of ours was populated in 1950. The figure of
7.5 billion for the year 2000 is a hypothetical one; the prob-
abilities of its realization are not high. It should be noted,
however, that the year 2000 is not remote in biological definition. All persons who will be thirty-five years old or older at the
end of the century are already born.

The validity of the projection to the year 2000 as an
estimate of the actual population in that year will not be
discussed in detail here. The estimates of the United Nations
are minimal; the probable population of the world under
assumptions of continuing trends is larger than the figure
cited. It is obvious that the world could support a population
of almost 8 billion or more in the year 2000—given full
utilization of the science, technology, and managerial know-
how now available. Realism may not accord with possibilities,
though. Whether or not India could absorb a further
increase of half a billion people in the next four decades is
debatable.

We could present and discuss estimated present and projected future populations for Asia on assumptions of continuing trends. We shall not do so for two major reasons.
First, and most significantly, there is no Asian future, nor is it
likely that there will be one in demographic levels, transformations, and associations. Second, the diversities in trends
within Asia are so intermingled with conjecture and estimate,
particularly for China, that neither the Chinese nor the Asian
future nor the East Asian-South Asian comparison can be

tions of continuing decline in mortality, is the initial level of the
birth rate. Since there are not now and never have been nationwide
birth and death rates of plausibility, and since age distributions are
similarly lacking, there is no consensus as to the probable level of the
birth rate, either in the Republic of China or today.

grounded in the logic of comparable projection procedures from closely estimated presents. The problem, of course, is the level of ignorance with reference to the population of mainland China.

The countries of South Asia can be considered together if the focus is the relationship of economic, social, and demographic trends. The region is also significant if the focus involves the relations between population factors and the maintenance of the peace. The immensity of the problems of population growth and the urgency of the search for solutions are apparent in the estimated future population of South Asia on the assumption of continuity in trends from 1960 to 2000. Since the population was so large in 1960, initially rapid and continually increasing rates of growth produce very large numbers over fairly brief periods of time. The population was 858 million in 1960. If death rates continue to decline and birth rates remain unchanged, the population would be 2.6 billion in 2000. Population in 2000 would be three times what it had been in 1960. South Asia alone in 2000 would have a population larger than that of the entire earth in 1950.

Past and Projected Growth in South Asia: 1920–2000

Present vulnerabilities associated with lagging food production suggest the hazards of projecting declining death rates and unchanging birth rates while populations already large increase at the rates and magnitudes of those in South Asia. Such projections may also be unrealistic. The forces of change are operative from the remote villages to provincial and central governments and international organizations. For South Asia the most plausible future populations involve declining fertility. An incisive view of the problems and possibilities for the future is given by tracing the population from 1920 to 1960 on the basis of actual growth, and then from 1960 to 2000 on the basis of projections that imply a reduction of the birth rates in most of the countries to half their original levels within this period. It is further assumed in the figures below that death rates move slowly downward from 1960 to 2000.

	Population (millions)	Growth (per cent)
1920	470	. .
1930	529	13
1940	610	15
1950	697	14
1960	858	23
1970	1,090	27
1980	1,366	25
1990	1,677	23
2000	2,023	21

The simple figures of the increasing numbers of people decade by decade from 1920 to 1960 suggest the human achievement in limiting the forces of death. From 1920 to 1960 the Malthusian scourges were gradually removed from the South Asian scene. From 1947 onward the organized services and campaigns, the increasing food production, and food supplies imported from abroad permitted quickening rates of growth as byproducts of declining death rates. The combination of a major technological impact on mortality and a relatively unchanging fertility produced the actual populations of 1960 and the potentials for growth thereafter.

The growth from 470 million in 1920 to 858 million in 1960 has occurred. There were almost 400 million more people in South Asia in 1960 than there had been four decades earlier.

The growth from 858 million in 1960 to 2.0 billion in 2000 is projected only. The increase of more than a billion population in South Asia in four decades has not yet occurred. Will it occur? Can death rates be preserved on downward courses in the various countries as populations and subsistence requirements mount? Can birth rates decline soon and continuously if population growth itself slows the rate of economic development and the speed of educational advance? These are the major questions of the South Asian, the Asian, and the world future.

Whether or not demographic transitions to low mortality and declining fertility occur in the next few decades in South Asian countries is not a question whose answers lie solely in demographic analysis. Increase of the magnitude of that projected requires internal stability and international order, increasing economic productivity to sustain the increasing numbers, social change to alter traditional family aspirations and value structures, and scientific advances in fertility control somewhat comparable to those that have already occurred in mortality control. All these difficult and diverse developments are required if the populations of the future are to correspond roughly to those that are projected.

Transformations and Transitions in Asia

If death rates are to decline to lower levels, there must be food, health facilities, and sanitation in more adequate form for larger portions of the people. If birth rates are to move downward, there must be social change, altered value structures, and an integration of population with economic and social developments in the plans, projects, and programs of governments. The unsponsored transitions of industrialization, urbanization, and education may occur in some limited areas of the Asian region. Some have occurred in the past; some are now occurring.

For most countries such transitions would be too limited and too late. In the past there were evasion and procrastination in the fundamental issue of government activities to reduce birth rates along with death rates. Increasing numbers of the governments of Asian countries now know that further delay may involve major hazards to the welfare if not the survival of citizens and to the internal strength and external power of the state.

India under the statesmanship of Prime Minister Nehru was the first of the large and populous countries to integrate population control into national planning. The Indian experience of the last decade has indicated not alone to India but to other countries and to population analysts the immensity of the task of reducing birth rates in traditional societies. Some declines in birth rates have been observed in some experimental or study situations. If there has been decline in the national birth rate it is too limited to be measurable in the rough vital statistics that are available. Death rates continued to decline from 1951 to 1961. The malaria eradication programs of recent years have been and are being spectacularly successful. Increases in food production lag, if indeed per-capita production is increasing at all. The equalization of opportunities and the lowering of the barriers in social structure proceed slowly. Given the population increase and the economic and social lethargies, the educational advances that might be stimulants to social change and economic productivity also lag. On the one hand, the interlocked changes that might accelerate in development are muted. On the other hand, the forces that might spiral downward in retrogression have been stayed.

Indian response to the crisis of the present involves a major re-emphasis of the population control program, with more intensive educational and motivational activities along with alternate and more effective means. The responses of various Asian countries to population growth are quite diverse. Some approach solutions to problems of population through actions designed to reduce birth rates. Others define problems of population growth as maldistribution, particularly that between densely settled central and sparsely settled peripheral areas.

In the Philippines and Indonesia there are mirages of frontier developments as direct solutions to problems of population growth, without numerical balancing of the relations between the amount of the growth in the settled areas, the costs of transfers, and the absorptive capacity of the presumptive settlement areas. In the Philippines the coincidence of a rate of population growth that approaches 4 per cent a year, mounting food deficits, and evidence that Mindanao is effectively occupied are beginning to force consideration of the interrelations of economic and demographic realities. In Indonesia the illusion of transmigration to the other islands as solution for Java remains, while the demographic situation becomes increasingly precarious.

There are areas of low birth rates in Asia. The fact of Japan requires no emphasis here. This is a country where a century of modernization has terminated in advanced demographic dynamics comparable to those in the countries of Western Europe. Birth rates are far below replacement needs; rural and urban fertility differentials are minimal. There may be need for governmental population policy to influence births, but if so the purpose is the restoration of fertility to maintenance levels.

There are countries with declining fertility in East Asia, but

they are so distinctive in characteristics that wider relevance
can be determined only after further study. The areas of
definitely established or presumptive decline include the Ryu-
kyu Islands (Japan's Okinawa prefecture), Taiwan, Hong
Kong, and the Chinese of Singapore and Malaya. All are areas
of economic development, with populations that are Chinese
or Chinese-related in ethnic origin and culture. In each instance, war, population movements, institutional changes, and
instabilities may have altered basic attitudes, aspirations, and
securities in ways conducive to altered marital, family, and
reproductive behavior.

The great questions of fertility change in Asia below the
Soviet Union concern levels, differentiations, and changes in
the Peoples Republics, particularly mainland China. Sparsity
of data precludes other than a conjectural consideration that
would not be appropriate here. There is also Soviet Asia,
where presently available data would permit analyses of the
dynamics of rural and urban populations in the various regions
along with comparisons of populations that are ethnically and
culturally European with the minorities that are Asian.

ECAFE and the United Nations

The diversities in Asia are basic to population theory, to the
analysis of population dynamics, and to the continental out-
look for political stability and peace. These diversities may
become stimulants to change rather than divisive forces if the
regional approach to cooperation in development becomes a
priority part of the activities of the Economic Commission for
Asia and the Far East. The initial conference of governments
to consider problems of population and to make recommendations was Asian in initiation, although the Bureau of Social

Affairs and other sectors of the United Nations cooperated in sponsorship and execution. The Asian Population Conference was held in New Delhi, India, December 1963. As noted, the primary sponsorship was that of ECAFE. Two aspects of this conference had major and perhaps coordinate significance:

1. The reiteration by U. Nyun, the executive secretary of ECAFE, that population growth was an Asian problem for Asian solution.

2. The unanimous resolutions recognizing the widely ramified nature of population problems, adjustments, and solutions; encouraging governments to assess the needs for policy; and recommending technical assistance, workshops, and other cooperative efforts under ECAFE auspices.

The recommendations of the Asian Population Conference formed the basis for resolutions in the meeting of ECAFE in Teheran in March 1964. These, in turn, were considered by the Economic and Social Council of the United Nations in August 1964. The General Assembly of the United Nations will again consider population growth and economic development at its forthcoming session.

Several of the Asian countries have developed governmental programs in the population field. The organizations of the United Nations system are evaluating the population problems of the member nations and assessing the appropriate roles of the international associations in their resolution. Speculation as to the date and type of further developments would be premature today. Three developments or postponements will indicate something as to the imminence of transformations in the United Nations system.

1. The actions of the General Assembly when it again considers the interrelations of population growth and economic development.

2. The extent of the integration of population work in the United Nations' secretariat at a level commensurate with its importance and appropriate to effective activity in research, technical assistance, and central service.

3. The movements in the United Nations system, particularly the World Health Organization.

Population, Development, and Peace

The interrelations of population growth, economic development, and social modernization are close. The associations of these various factors with the preservation of the peace and the incidence of conflict are little studied in the context of the world as it now exists. The specific question involves the relations of population to peace in Asia. The answer would require intricate, comprehensive, and multidisciplinary analysis. The scope would be wide, for powers and developments outside Asia are involved as well as those within Asia. The interrelations would be complex, for there are confrontations of the Peoples Republics and other countries as well as confrontations within each of the political and ideological groupings. Ancient problems persist alongside the new; nationalism has been added to, substituted for, or intermingled with ethnic, religious, and other subcultural conflicts.

The research required for generalization as to the role of population factors in stability and change, acceptance and insurrection, peace and war must involve case studies of the interrelations of demographic and political factors. Since this research has not been done and is not in process, general comments substitute for analytical résumés.

Any considerations of the relations of population to peace in Asia must have as preface a note on the politics of population and the role of demographic mythologies in political arguments. Population pressure and population increase are widely prevalent explanations for internal insurrection, external expansion, and war. It would be just as plausible to assign the increasing pressures of population, the mounting misery, and the conflict to the economic stagnation, the rigidities of class structures, or the political maladjustments. Population may be a preferred villain because it is more simply presented and seemingly more immutable than economic and social factors. Neither governments nor controlling institutions need be blamed for demographic difficulties. Solutions need not be sought in economic reorganization, institutional reforms, or altered values and ideals in social and political ethics.

Population growth is also an argument of propriety for a government that would hesitate to present power as the goal of specific activities, whether political, economic, or military. The classic instance is the Japanese argument of population pressure; the classic Japanese case is the use of the plea of land for the peasants of overpopulated Japan in the imperialist venture that removed the land of Manchuria from China. The complexities of analysis are further compounded by the fact that many Japanese politicians, administrators, and even professional personnel believed the demographic arguments that were cited as the forces impelling military action.

There is another mythology that must be listed as one of the relationships between population and peace. The prevalent belief that population can be equated with power may be untrue. Whatever the facts, the belief blocks a rational consideration of population growth as an aspect of the economic problems of a country. The belief in the associations of population and power may be a factor in the generation of

pressures that lead to internal instabilities or the resort to
external action.

There is a persuasive case for the associations of severe
population pressure and insurgency. The Huk activities in the
rice areas of central Luzon, the rebel activities against the
Dutch in Java, the revolution in the Tonkin delta of Indo-
China, the problem of refugees and central government control in East Pakistan—all these focused in areas where people
were settled densely on the land and pressures were being
accentuated by population growth. However, the argument of
identity between population pressure and rebellion or sub-
version would require instability or insurrection in all subareas
of equivalent pressure throughout Asia, and only within these
areas. This relationship could hardly be sustained.

The ancient and the modern alike characterize many of the
associations of population and peace in Asia. Population
growth, communist ideologies, and national expansionist goals
are intermingled in the perpetuation of the traditional processes of recurrent conflict and accommodation. The tribal or
nomad frontiers with the settled agriculturalists were critical
in the history of Asia. They remain so today, whether in
China, Indo-China, or the Pakistan-Afghan area. Similarly,
ethnic, religious, and linguistic diversities where hostilities
are latent may erupt in violent action when the pressures of
mounting population intensify the hostilities and mitigate
the cautions.

The global questions of the Asian future involve population
in emerging power relationships. The fundamental fact is the
disharmony between the distribution of population and the
distribution of the resources essential either to the further
development of agricultural production or the transition to
the modern industrial state with its advanced technologies.

This problem would exist in Asia whatever the timing of the move to modernization and whatever the political affiliations at the time the drives to modernization began. Given the delayed modernization, the synchronization of nationalist awakening and communist political advance, and the coincidence of both these with the scientific and technological advances in mortality control, Asia's problems of population, development, and war become hazards not alone to Asia but to the world.

The three great problems of the Asian future may be mentioned in order of ascending priorities as conclusion to this brief discussion of a topic so fundamental that its continuing neglect is quite incomprehensible. The first is the contiguity of the river basins of Southeast Asia with their vast potentialities for food production and power with the massive populations for whom food deficiencies are threats to welfare and to internal stability. The second is the renewal of the historic expansion of the Han people, now as the outward movement of a developing, militaristic, and ideologically motivated state under extreme tensions associated with its multitudinous and increasing people. The third and ultimately the most ominous problem is the juxtaposition of the northern reaches of Soviet Asia where resources are abundant, population sparse, technologies advanced, and people European with the southern reaches of the continent where resources are limited, people abundant, technologies retarded, and people Asian.

NEED FOR CATHOLIC ACTION

JOHN L. THOMAS, S.J.

Our belated awareness of the far-reaching individual and institutional implications of contemporary world population trends is bound to put us under something of an emotional strain. We had assumed that our rapid scientific advances would enable us, at long last, to release mankind from its agelong struggle for mere subsistence. We had some knowledge that many members of the "Third World," the roughly two-thirds of our fellow men living in economically underdeveloped countries, were still facing hunger, malnutrition, or numerous deprivations. Michael Harrington's *The Other America* had alerted us to the surprising nature and extent of the poverty concealed in our own society of abundance.

Nonetheless, we had come to believe that science would offer ample means for satisfying man's material needs, provided we were prepared to use it. It is indeed upsetting to learn that bread alone—or even cake—is not enough. We are again confronted with the old Malthusian dilemma, though its dimensions are radically changed.

Were this experience of emotional strain to arouse us to active involvement, it could prove salutary indeed, particularly here in America; though, as Barbara Ward has recently warned us, one of the penalties of affluence is that nothing quite succeeds in biting through the layers of expected comfort and accepted ease. We have need to feel serious concern,

concern that will stimulate the active search for more adequate knowledge and the careful development of more discriminating judgments. To be sure, a mass of global statistics is now available, but we are just beginning to identify clearly the dimensions of our knowledge and of our ignorance regarding both the relevant historical facts and the complex interrelationships existing among the demographic, economic, social, and cultural factors involved in contemporary population dynamics.

The aim of this study is twofold: to discuss some of the special reasons why American Catholics should become actively interested in contemporary population problems, and to indicate some of the necessary considerations that should guide their approach in formulating policy proposals under current conditions of pluralism. I shall proceed on the assumption that significant population problems exist and that their general demographic features are sufficiently well known. Since several aspects of the historical context within which these problems developed appear relevant to our discussion, however, I shall begin with a few observations relating to the historical background of the present situation.

The Historical Context of Modern Population Control

Contrary to what one might conclude from the writing of some population theorists of the past few centuries, the general attitude of the Church during the first stages of development and throughout the Middle Ages cannot be characterized as pro-populationist. Christian thought held virginity in very high esteem, strongly encouraged celibacy, and imposed severe controls on the uses of marriage. Church teaching and discipline, nevertheless, by inculcating a profound respect for life and the order of nature, gradually succeeded in creating a general climate of opinion within which infanticide, abortion, sterilization, contraception, sexual perversions, and various unusual marital practices came to be regarded as "unnatural" and were consequently condemned as seriously immoral ways of interfering with the Creator's plan expressed in the natures of things.

Such forbidden practices were not thought of in terms of population control, however, for it was uniformly assumed that their use was prompted primarily by hedonistic motives and in most cases constituted nothing more than an attempt to inhibit or destroy the natural product of illicit sexual activities. Since infant mortality rates remained high and the economic costs of raising children were relatively minor throughout this period, most couples apparently felt little inclination to question the order of nature by limiting the size of their families.

Evidence that traditional attitudes toward family size and the passive acceptance of the natural course of events were undergoing change first appeared around the end of the sixteenth century. This new trend would grow steadily during subsequent centuries as various scientific and social developments generated increasing concern with maternal and infant health care, social mobility, higher standards of living, and, above all, with that lengthened training and formal education of children associated with the emergence of the modern family and constituting its most characteristic note. Although the effective limitation of family size proceeded at different rates and followed somewhat different lines in various Western countries, the basic pattern varied little. Beginning first among the upper classes and then gradually diffusing downward, attitudes and knowledge relating to various methods of birth control, formerly confined largely to social deviants, or members of the demimonde, became an integral element of Western family culture.

Two aspects of this historical development are relevant to our discussion. First, for the most part, the initial rapid diffusion and widespread acceptance of objectionable birth-control practices in the Western world took place without benefit of clergy, significant secular leadership, or well-organized public propaganda. Once the pressure of changing circumstances generated the effective desire to limit family size, individual couples took matters into their own hands and had recourse to various publicly disapproved practices. Because this silent revolution constituted a threat to established family and sexual mores, it was strongly contested and roundly condemned by religious and secular leaders alike. This aura of official disapproval has remained, even though this revolution gradually gained some measure of respectability after making its appearance as an organized social movement in various countries. What is more important, this atmosphere of conflict and contention, associated particularly with the organized movements, has had the unfortunate effect of diverting concern from basic issues and focusing attention on the promotion or defeat of relatively short-range, segmented programs.

Second, perhaps because this silent revolution and its subsequent movements embodied so many morally objectionable traits, the major interest and energy of religious leaders were expended on these obvious targets. Hence these leaders failed to analyze the real nature and underlying causes of the revolutionary shift in family and sexual mores that they were witnessing. Yet it should have been obvious that traditional interpretations of sex, love, and marriage were no longer capable of supplying a meaningful moral framework within which effective ways of meeting the changed exigencies of parenthood under contemporary conditions could be developed.

The failure of religious leaders to recognize the implications of this fact and to develop workable solutions forced couples facing the nonpostponable daily needs of family life to rely on their own solutions. As a review of evolving population patterns in the Western world clearly indicates, once couples became sufficiently determined to limit family size they were capable of discovering effective ways to accomplish this purpose. The means they used were necessarily related to available resources—technical, psychological, social, and spiritual. History shows that delayed marriages, celibacy, marital continence, contraception, sterilization, abortion, and even veiled infanticide—conveniently disguised under the cloak of child abandonment, as during the eighteenth and nineteenth centuries in Europe—all came to be used more or less effectively and extensively at one time or another.

The central fact that must be kept in mind if we would grasp the real significance of modern population problems is that owing to a series of developments that began around the sixteenth century, and which we may loosely summarize under the term industrialization, Western man's traditional relationship to reproduction has undergone marked changes. The profound implications of this fact have been partially obscured in the industrialized nations of the West because various forms of birth control have been effectively employed to reduce birth rates. Thus no major Western nation has solved its population problems by using methods to which the Church would give moral approval.

It is indeed difficult to conjecture what forms practical

solutions based on morally approved methods would assume under present conditions. Clearly they would involve later age at marriage, perhaps relatively high rates of celibacy, and the widespread observance of either absolute or periodic continence during considerable portions of fertile couples' reproductive spans. At any rate, problems of population control have not received morally approved solutions in the West, and realism demands that we keep this in mind when discussing programs relating to current world population trends.

The Catholic Minority in Historical Perspective

Whether it is owing primarily to widespread religious indifference, the extensive social mobility of Catholics, or the increasing significance of urban centers in which the Church has always been strong, it appears that American Catholics are gradually achieving some measure of national acceptance and are now moving toward the assumption of greater responsibility in shaping social and cultural trends. A religious minority's sphere and scope of social influence are always conditioned by its history. What American Catholics can do will depend to some extent upon what they have done, for they are currently enriched or impoverished by past successes or failures and bound by past decisions or commitments that may limit their areas of choice in the present.

Moreover, since social goals and practical programs of action necessarily embody definite premises of values, members of a religious minority cherishing a distinctive set of moral principles and values face a difficult task when cooperating with others in formulating public policy. Such cooperation requires an atmosphere of mutual understanding and respect, and, at best, in making public policy decisions under conditions of pluralism, it is never easy to distinguish reasons required by the common good from those based on religious convictions. If a religious minority is relatively small, loosely integrated, or lacking in social prestige and power, its primary concern may prudently be focused on religious survival rather than on influencing public policy.

For a variety of reasons this latter approach was adopted by the Catholic minority in this country until a few decades ago. Starting as a scattered handful of perhaps thirty-five thousand in the late eighteenth century, the Church's remarkable growth up to 1925, at least, was the result primarily of several major waves of immigration. Their distinctive immigrant origins had far-reaching consequences for members of the Catholic minority. Faced with relative hostility and discrimination from without the Church and little understanding or appreciation of national differences from within, the new arrivals directed their major efforts toward securing a living and preserving cherished ethnic practices and values. All that the majority of them asked was an opportunity to work and to be left alone. Clustered around their parishes in the industrial areas of the East and Great Lakes regions, they were largely content to let others run the country. If they took any interest in politics, it was primarily for protection. National and local leaders lost few opportunities to remind them that this was a Protestant country. Confronted with a national image they were little prepared to challenge, the various ethnic segments of the Catholic minority fell back upon their own resources in seeking means to assure their survival. The magnificent system of churches, schools, and charitable institutions they established clearly attests their energy, resourcefulness, and conviction.

Because American Catholics have long regarded themselves

as a merely tolerated minority, they tend to become quite defensive when accused of failure to assume adequate responsibility for the promotion of local community or national welfare. Up until recently many remained not a little skeptical about trying to influence public policy through the democratic process. Although conscious of their increasing strength in numbers, they were inclined to agree with Dennis Brogan's 1944 statement that "the American public, the American politician, the American newspaper has to allow for Catholic opinion because there are so many Catholics, not because Catholic opinion has any interest as such."

It is now generally recognized that this partly enforced, partly self-imposed attitude of quasi-alienation represented only a temporary stage of adjustment as members of the Catholic minority moved toward full participation in community affairs, yet its roots are deep in the past and some of its effects can still be observed. To cite a few examples relevant to the present discussion, although informed Catholics are aware of their right and obligation to render public witness to the truth as they see it, some fail to recognize that moral principles or premises of values do not in themselves constitute practical programs of action. Thus when definite social problems are found to exist, they cannot be solved by the mere assertion of general moral principles, since these become meaningful only when they are implemented by or translated into concrete social relationships. Nor is it a mark of responsible citizenship to rest content with merely opposing every program based on morally objectionable premises, for such a negative approach obviously leaves the real problem unsolved.

Moreover, because past public policy proposals involving objectionable birth-control measures have usually carried heavy political and social as well as moral overtones, Catholics

have tended to counter them primarily by exerting appropriate
social and political pressures. As a result of this short-range, *ad
hoc* approach, which may or may not have been justified in the
past, Catholics have given too little consideration to the
far-reaching, practical implications of living under conditions
of pluralism. As all who must deal with public welfare proposals regarding population control soon discover, the
Church's position has not yet been clarified, and there is still
little agreement concerning the moral values and principles
that should be considered relevant in formulating a Catholic
approach.

With these observations in mind, let us now turn to the
special reasons why American Catholics should become actively interested in contemporary population problems. I take
it for granted that Catholics, as citizens of a resource-adequate
country, share equal responsibility with their fellow citizens in
promoting programs designed to aid resource-needy nations,
and consequently I shall confine my remarks to those elements
in the present situation that should be of special concern to
Catholics. These may be briefly summarized as follows:

First, starting at home, since the history of family regulation
in the United States indicates that, with few exceptions, the
emerging pattern relating to family size is well below the
biological potential of fertile couples, Catholics must recognize this situation and be prepared to deal with it. Second, at
the theoretical level, although Western man's changed relationship to reproduction has far-reaching implications for
traditional conceptions of sex, love, and marriage, these have
not yet been faced by Catholics or others. Third, at the
practical level, if they would not betray their Christian heritage, Catholics must clarify their attitudes regarding public

policy relating to local, national, and international problems of population control.

Family Regulation in the United States

Studies based on both official government data and special research in the field give us a good deal of information concerning the reproductive pattern of the American people, although we have only limited knowledge of the causal factors involved in the long-run secular trends and various sub-group differences revealed. The fertility of the American people from the time of the first permanent settlements to the early decades of the nineteenth century was among the world's highest. It is estimated that during this period of more than two centuries women of completed fertility had an average of about eight children. Since the beginning of the nineteenth century, however, the fertility history of the United States may be characterized as one of relatively rapid transition from large families to small. For example, from 1810 to 1940 the decennial censuses show a virtually uninterrupted decline in the ratio of young children under five to 1,000 white women twenty to forty-four years old (from 1,358 to 419, or 939 points). The bulk of this decline occurred in the nineteenth century (about 29 per cent before 1840 and 70 per cent before 1900), and was the result of falling birth rates among both urban and rural families.

Because increases in the number of women of childbearing age more than offset the effect of the declining birth rate per woman, the annual number of births increased elevenfold between 1800 (280,000) and 1921 (about 3.1 million). After this date there was a gradual decline to a low of 2.3 million in

1933; then followed a slow increase to 1940 (2.6 million); a sharp but fluctuating increase during the war years; and record increases after 1945, reaching an annual average of somewhat over 4 million during the last ten years. Although the crude birth rate (births per 1,000 population) has declined steadily since 1957, this does not in itself indicate a decline in *fertility*, for the number of women currently available for childbearing is relatively smaller (women born during the late twenties and the depression years).

It seems reasonable to infer the gradual spread of family limitation practices from: (1) the long-run secular decline in fertility; (2) the negative correlation of fertility and social status as measured by occupation, education, or income throughout the prewar years; (3) the higher fertility of the rural population; (4) the lack of relationship between completed family size and changes in the age at marriage and the spacing of children; and (5), the contemporary trend toward the contraction of most of the traditional fertility differentials by occupation, education, income, or residence—with the result that there seems to be an emerging consensus on family size throughout most of the population.

An analysis of the baby boom that started in 1946 indicates that it was affected by the following elements: (1) in the initial stage, a making-up-for babies postponed in the depression and war years; (2) a shift in the timing of marriages and births to earlier stages independently of the changes in completed family size; (3) a considerable increase in the proportion marrying; and (4) an apparent shift from very small to moderate size for completed families among the married.

In other words, there now appears to be little or no voluntary childlessness, while the increase in average family size seems to be the result primarily of more births of the first to fourth orders. Whether this trend will persist is far from certain; indeed, some findings of recent field studies suggest that the desired family size among young couples is beginning to decline, and as the Princeton Family Studies show, the desired number of children appears to be one of the best single predictors of subsequent fertility.

We have no adequate information on the fertility history of American Catholics and consequently cannot document the changes that may have occurred. Judging from numerous studies on desired family size and reports on actual reproductive performance, however, we may safely conclude that among practicing Catholic couples fertility is higher than among Protestants, Jews, and others, while all religious groups have apparently adjusted their reproductive patterns to similar environmental changes in the same direction, although this reaction is less marked among Catholics than others. Thus Catholic couples follow the current trend of marrying earlier than in the past, even though it is estimated that they still marry considerably later than Protestants; the majority of Catholic couples tend to desire family size below normal biological potential, but significantly larger than other couples; and compared class for class, with the exception of couples at the lowest socioeconomic levels, they tend to have larger completed families than others.

For information on the nature and extent of family limitation practices we must rely on special field studies. The pioneering Indianapolis Study of the Social and Psychological Factors Affecting Fertility (1941) revealed that, among the urban native-white Protestant couples with complete grammar-school education or more, over 98 per cent of the "relatively fecund" couples (860) and about two-thirds of the "relatively sterile" couples (220) reported some past experience with contraception. About two-thirds of the couples began contraception at marriage and five-sixths had started before the end of the first puerperium. The study did not investigate contraceptive practices among Catholics, but the household survey conducted preliminary to the subsequent intensive study indicated that Catholic couples had higher fertility than Protestants, and also that socioeconomic differentials in fertility were more marked among the Protestants than among the Catholic couples.

The important Growth of American Families research (GAF) based on a scientific probability sample (2,713) of all white married women between the ages of eighteen and thirty-nine inclusive living in the United States in March 1955, reveals the almost universal use of some form of family limitation practices by fecund couples.[1] Thus, 90 per cent of the fecund couples with wives aged thirty to thirty-nine had already used preventive measures. Most of the couples who had not used them were subfecund (limited in their ability to have children) and did not need them. Among the 787 Catholic couples studied, 43 per cent had made no attempt to limit family size, 27 per cent had used rhythm only, and the remaining 30 per cent had used methods unacceptable to the Church. However, among the fecund Catholic couples married at least ten years, 50 per cent had used a method other than rhythm.

Another significant finding of this study was that 9 per cent of all couples—one in eleven—had had an operation which made conception impossible. In other words, most of the 10

[1] Ronald Freedman, Pascal K. Whelpton, and Arthur A. Campbell, *Family Planning, Sterility and Population Growth*. New York: McGraw-Hill, 1959.

per cent of couples found to be definitely sterile had had such an operation. Undoubtedly some of these operations were contraceptive in intent, and in this connection it is interesting to note that only 6 per cent of Catholic couples were definitely sterile as compared to 12 per cent of Protestants. Although Catholic couples in the study had the same average number of births as Protestant couples (2.1), they had married later and their current reproductive performance suggested that their completed family size would probably be larger (3.5 as opposed to 3.0).

The Princeton two-child family study[2] further documents the widespread extent of family limitation practices—only 11 per cent of the total sample report having never used contraception up to the time of the interview (five or six months after having had the second child). Among Catholic couples in the sample, however, 22 per cent of the white-collar class and 17 per cent of the blue-collar class were nonusers. Judging from the findings of this study and its follow-up three years later in 1960, when 905 of the original 1,165 couples were reinterviewed,[3] it appears that the amount of Catholic education, particularly after high school, is strongly and directly related to the number of children desired, while the desired number of children is the best single predictor of subsequent fertility.

On the basis of the research cited above and other more specialized studies, we may conclude that family limitation is now almost universally approved and is practiced widely and

[2] Charles F. Westoff, Robert G. Potter, Jr., Philip C. Sagi, and Elliot G. Mishler, *Family Growth in Metropolitan America*. Princeton: Princeton University Press, 1961.

[3] Charles F. Westoff, Robert G. Potter, Jr., and Philip C. Sagi, *The Third Child*. Princeton: Princeton University Press, 1963.

effectively by the white couples who need it. With the probable exception of that 10 per cent found in the lower socioeconomic class, the majority of all classes of the American population are coming to share a common set of values about family size; and though marked religious differences in fertility values still exist, in the sense that Catholics want and expect more children than Protestants, the differences tend to approach the range of variation prescribed by the prevailing cultural norm of two to four children. However, within the Catholic minority and in contrast to the general population, couples in the white-collar class tend to have higher fertility than couples in the blue-collar class, and couples with a Catholic college background are least likely to desire small families and most likely to employ periodic continence to achieve the family size desired if regulation is required.

Thus we may conclude that owing to early age at marriage, extensive emphasis on sexual stimulation and expression, high standards of maternal and infant health care, and added length of formal preparation required to prepare children for adequate participation in a technologically advanced society, most fertile young American couples are faced with the serious challenge of spacing pregnancies and regulating the size of their families. As members of a morally pluralist society, however, Catholic couples must solve their family problem within a framework of beliefs, values, and norms no longer recognized as valid by most of their contemporaries. This means that they must work out their solutions within a social system geared to the small family and operating on the assumption that contraceptive birth control will be extensively employed. Since this key solution is unacceptable to Catholic couples, the entire web of their premarital, marital, and family relationships must be restructured accordingly.

Implications of Man's Changed Relationship
to Reproduction

Although the imbalance between rapidly expanding numbers and underdeveloped natural resources currently occurring in most of the large agrarian societies of the world constitutes an immediate challenge that must not be ignored, it does not in itself reveal the true nature of our contemporary population problems. Western man has already indicated that, when adequately motivated, he is quite capable of family limitation and even wasteful overproduction. Obviously, the search for more reliable and acceptable means of population control, together with more efficient methods of exploiting all the resources of nature, must be relentlessly pursued; but success in this pursuit alone will not solve the fundamental human issues resulting from the changes in man's traditional relationship to reproduction that are implied.

To state this thesis briefly, since concern with reproduction, considered in terms of both individual fulfillment and social continuity, constitutes one of the major wellsprings of organization and motivation in all human societies, changes that radically affect man's relationship to reproduction will have profound repercussions on his total conduct of life and consequently require careful rethinking and restructuring of all relevant human relationships. These changes have already occurred in the West and are gradually being introduced into most currently underdeveloped countries. In this connection, I might suggest that the reluctance of many couples in these societies to limit family size is not owing to their indifference to hunger, sickness, and suffering but indicates that their interrelated systems of social organization and motivation, traditionally geared to unrestricted procreation, have not yet been sufficiently affected by change to make family limitation meaningful to most couples.

As has been indicated, the far-reaching implications of Western man's changed status regarding reproduction have remained largely unexamined, although we find increasing evidence of frustration, normlessness, and growing incapacity to find more than passing physical significance in the personally and socially crucial area of sex relations. The restricted procreation and limited family size now being practiced and more or less universally required in the foreseeable future raise serious questions concerning the adequacy of traditional conceptions of sex, love, and marriage. Why must there be an essential relationship between sex and procreation? To what extent are primarily non-procreative marital relations capable of maintaining the unity of the monogamous couple? How does family limitation affect cultural attitudes and practices regarding parenthood? What solutions can be offered for the increasing ambivalence of woman's role under conditions of limited motherhood? What are the implications of small family size for parental roles and the balanced development of children?

These questions are only a few of those which suggest themselves, but they are sufficient to indicate the major dimensions of the challenge we face. Clearly what is needed, therefore, is a thorough reinterpretation, based on Christian premises of values, of the personal and social significance of human sexuality, together with a careful restructuring of the various relationships relevant to its meaningful development, expression, and regulation. This approach must include the well-reasoned formulation of an integrated view of human sexuality, a formulation that would take into account both the complementary character of its psychophysical, psychosocial, and spiritual attributes, together with the various stages of sexual growth in the process of personality development, and also the individual and institutional implications of its function as unique means of expressing human love and creativity. The contributions of religion, philosophy, and the various medical and social sciences are required here, for no single discipline is adequate for dealing with the complex phenomena involved; yet the point to be emphasized is that the essential challenge of modern population trends is not primarily explosive numbers or scarce resources but the reformulation and cultural implementation of a conception of human sexuality consonant with the destiny of the person and the needs of society under modern conditions.

The Catholic Position and Public Policy

A further reason why Catholics should take an active interest in population problems is their need to clarify their position relating to various public population policy proposals involving birth-control measures. Since all practical programs of action embody definite premises of values, in a morally pluralist society like our own the formulation of acceptable value premises relating to publicly supported programs of population control becomes a formidable task. Members of a pluralist society have the right and the obligation to render witness to the truth as they see it. Since their public policy decisions must be determined by the current exigencies of the common good, however, they must realistically consider to what extent human procreative activities should be subjected to public controls, what public programs are feasible under existing conditions, and to what extent a given program provides for the freedom of conscience of all responsible citizens.

Recent concern with population problems at home and abroad had led to the introduction of various birth-control measures in both local welfare and international assistance programs, and perhaps no issue has brought home more sharply to the American people the serious implications of moral pluralism. The general principle that public policy decisions must be determined by reasons derived from the exigencies of the common good, rather than by reasons based on individual religious convictions, is clear enough in theory, but it obscures the significant fact that conceptions of many elements of the common good are largely determined by one's religious convictions.

This statement merits further consideration. Although there is general awareness that the family system embraced by Catholics, for example, involves distinctive normative aspects relating to the nature of the marital bond, the purposes of marriage, the functions of sex, and so on, the fact that these distinctive aspects result from the logical application of sets of socially relevant conceptions or propositions of an identifiable religious derivation is frequently overlooked. Briefly, in any ongoing society the essential structure through which human social activities are directed, ordered, and integrated is constituted by the accepted sets of obligatory norms centering around the fulfilment of man's basic social needs—sexual, economic, political, and so forth. These norms may be viewed as directives for action, since they define the acceptable ways of doing things in a given society.

What is the source of the obligatory quality of such norms? These norms imply values, that is, goals or objectives that are considered worth striving for and to which the norms are related as means to ends. What is the source of the values embodied in these norms? Values are related to the beliefs concerning the nature of man and his world held by a given group. In this context, beliefs represent statements about the nature of reality, and in an integrated system of action they furnish the ultimate rationale for the values and ends embodied in the system's obligatory normative structure.

The Catholic religion, as all developed religious systems, offers, through its established creed, cult, and code, a set of beliefs concerning man's origin, his relationships to space and time, the essential qualities of his nature and consequently of his orientation to his fellow men, society, and the world of nature, and, finally, his life purpose. Inasmuch as it does so, it necessarily furnishes the basic beliefs underlying the normative family value orientations of American Catholics. On the other hand, because general moral principles can be logically applied to concrete social situations only after all the elements in the situation have been carefully analyzed, Catholic thinkers regard the ethical process—that is, the specific determination of the right ordering of man's individual and social life on the basis of his religious beliefs—as dynamic and existential in the sense that human reason, supplemented by principles derived from revelation and tradition, must formulate the Christian's pattern of moral decisions in terms of the changing necessities of the situation.

This means, of course, that although their religion furnishes relevant moral principles or starting points, American Catholics cannot deduce a priori from these principles the position they should take in regard to public programs involving objectionable birth-control measures. Moreover, since these programs include significant new moral issues, past experience provides few guiding precedents for present decision. Hence Catholics must study all aspects of these programs, together with the total situational contexts within which they function, before deciding whether to oppose them actively or tolerate them passively; whether to accept some elements and reject others; and whether they are prepared to propose workable alternatives or, from lack of such, to tolerate present programs as the lesser of two evils.

Some Guiding Considerations

For a number of reasons—sudden awareness of the nature and potential of contemporary population trends, man's seemingly endemic inability to deal rationally with sex, the historical context within which family limitation occurred, the perennial reluctance of the American people to face realistically the practical implications of moral pluralism—many proposed solutions to population problems tend to run toward what Alva Myrdal once characterized as remedial quackery. Denial that any general problem exists, trust in some vague type of providentialism, belief that some as yet unknown regulatory mechanisms in the human species will eventually become operative, panic-stricken insistence that birth rates must be lowered quickly by any means and at any costs, the use of veiled authoritarian coercion to impose specific methods, all fall in this category.

Since complex new problems exist, we cannot continue to preserve new wine in old wineskins, yet since profound human values are involved, we must be careful in our zeal to meet current needs, not to destroy what we would preserve. As I have pointed out, neither religious nor secular thinkers have yet come to grips with the far-reaching implications of the changes Western man's relationship to reproduction has been undergoing since the sixteenth century. Surely, the fact that couples in the West simply limited their family by any means available must not be interpreted as an authentic solution to the basic population problems we face.

Although no clear-cut solutions are available, I shall presume to suggest several considerations that seem particularly relevant to any realistic approach toward solutions consonant with Christian beliefs and values. I might add that, inasmuch as the development of valid solutions involves an adequate grasp of Catholic beliefs, an informed awareness of the relationships between these beliefs and relevant social values, and a trained ability not only to identify what principles are pertinent to the situation but also to apply such principles to the specific categories of human actions under consideration, we may conclude that only those individuals who have seriously studied the facts and pondered the principles will be prepared to make any worth-while contributions.

As a first consideration I submit that given current nuptiality rates, age at marriage, advances in health care, and so forth, no sizable modern nation could long make reasonable provision for its population increases if its people were to make use of their full reproductive capacity. Hence it seems inconceivable in the foreseeable future, at least, that couples in any major industrialized country will radically reverse the long-term trend toward small families by returning to unrestricted procreation. This means that family limitation in one form or another has become a significant element in modern culture, and short of radical new scientific developments in methods of control, attempts to control family size through contraceptives will continue to be associated with widespread use of sterilization and abortion.

Second, owing to the rather extensive failure of religious thinkers to recognize the practical implications of contemporary population trends, many fertile Catholic couples are experiencing serious problems which they are ill prepared to handle. During the last several years there has been some increasing awareness of the need for a morally acceptable, effective means of regulating family size, yet past reluctance to encourage and support competent research, instruction, and guidance on the practice of periodic continence has limited the availability and usefulness of this method for most Catholic couples. Lack of adequate instruction regarding the morality of rhythm and its relationship to conjugal spirituality has left many couples uncertain and confused; at the same time they have few reliable sources of information and guidance relating to the practical knowledge requisite for the effective use of this practice, since the majority even of Catholic physicians are not prepared to render competent service, though most apparently attempt to do so.

Third, although we have limited knowledge concerning the complex cultural processes through which human groups and individual couples are moved to restrict reproduction or to select one available means rather than another in doing so, experience shows that once social pressures are sufficiently high, and in the absence of acceptable alternatives, couples will resort to any means at hand. The relatively high rates of such seriously objectionable practices as sterilization, abortion, and even child abandonment occurring in some so-called Catholic cultures must be kept in mind when evaluating various public population policy proposals.

Fourth, thinking about foreign-aid programs and birth control, we should labor under no misconceptions regarding the difficulties and complexities of the problems involved. Functioning social systems are integrated systems, so that segmented, piecemeal reforms, such as public programs to lower the birth rate, will have little lasting effect. The immediate problem is how to promote the cultural transition required if people of underdeveloped countries are to be converted to rapid industrial development. These societies must choose between immediate conversion to an intensive industrial development or increasing poverty and decline. Popular American opinion to the contrary, piecemeal reforms, such as birth-control programs, are ineffective under the circumstances, both because they are not aimed at changing traditional social and economic conditions and because they cannot appeal effectively to couples until such changes occur. There are no facile solutions to the problems these countries face.

Fifth, in clarifying their position relative to various publicly supported welfare programs involving objectionable birth-control measures, Catholics must weigh the advantages of serving a prophetic mission in society by opposing such programs against the disadvantages of not participating in the formulation of public policy. The Church's attitude toward divorce legislation in this country may provide a case in point. Considering the present legislation, one may well question whether refusal to participate in its development has notably promoted the interests of the common good.

Finally, we must give serious thought to the fact that most of our urban centers and some of our rural slums now include an apparently increasing number of individuals who for a variety of reasons appear incapable of exercising responsible control of their sexual activities. Further, owing to the disorganized social conditions under which they must live, their lack of training and education, the undisciplined sexual mores of their associates, and the low mental caliber of some, there seems good reason to believe that they will not voluntarily make consistent use of any of the current forms of contraceptives. Since we have not yet discovered effective methods to assure the adequate rearing of the children resulting from these irresponsible activities, we are confronted with the problem of having to provide for a steadily increasing, irresponsible "inner proletariat." Perhaps our society can carry this burden with ease, yet it raises serious questions concerning the morally permissible measures the state may take to limit irresponsible procreation. If I read the signs of the times correctly, these questions merit immediate consideration.

Population Growth:
Some Economic Problems

Oscar Harkavy

The Secretary General of the United Nations recently asked the member nations to prepare extensive statements on "the reciprocal action of economic development and population change."[1] The government of Italy notes that the "interrelationships between population and economic phenomena are intricate and relevant theories highly controversial." I agree that there is need for much more sophisticated analysis by economists who know their demography, but I cannot concur with the conclusion expressed by the government of Italy and several other Western European countries that "present policy should provide for an adjustment of economic conditions to the demographic situation rather than an adaptation of population to economic conditions." I admit that this would be the preferable course of action if there were complete freedom of choice. But I believe that rapid growth of population stacks the odds against the developing countries of Asia, Africa, and Latin America as they struggle to release the mass of their citizens from poverty.

Investment in factories, agricultural improvement, roads,

[1] United Nations Economic and Social Council, "Inquiry Among Governments on Problems Resulting from the Reciprocal Action of Economic Development and Population Changes," E/3895, May 18, 1964, and June 30, 1964.

and technical education—the conventional instruments of economic development—must be accompanied by investment in national programs designed to reduce the birth rate if rising per capita income is to be achieved by the poor nations of the world. Referring again to the United Nations inquiry, the governments of Ceylon, Chile, Formosa, Guatemala, India, Iran, Jamaica, Jordan, Korea, Lebanon, Pakistan, Panama, the Philippines, Tunisia, Turkey, and the UAR express doubts whether they can satisfy the needs and aspirations of their people during the next decade in the face of rapid population growth.

Population Density

The picture that first comes to mind in confronting the "population explosion" is a mass of humanity, like rush-hour passengers in the New York subway, struggling for two square feet of standing room. But crowding is not necessarily associated with poverty. There are about 327 people per square mile in India and 21 people per square mile in Laos. Both have per capita income of about $80 a year. On the other hand, the megalopolis stretching from Boston to Washington has a population density of more than 2,000 per square mile, while enjoying a median family income of nearly $7,000 a year. Were this area dependent on agriculture or mining and unable to trade with the rest of the United States or with the rest of the world, 2,000 people crowded together on each square mile would be able to eke out but a miserable livelihood. To take another example, per capita income in Hong Kong, with a density of 8,000 per square mile, has risen 7 to 10 per cent a year since World War II. Despite a huge influx of refugees from mainland China, Hong Kong is one of the most prosperous countries in Asia because of its vigorous industry and world trade.[2]

Overcrowding is undesirable for many reasons. But those responsible for a nation's population policy will make a grave mistake if they focus exclusively on population density. Latin America, where one-fourteenth of the world's population lives on one-seventh of the world's land mass, does not suffer from "overpopulation" in terms of density per square mile. But Latin America faces major problems brought about by its high rate of population growth. It is hard pressed to provide adequate food, housing, and education for its children and productive employment for new entrants to the labor force. And, as I shall point out further on, the great proportion of dependent children in a fast-growing population is a heavy handicap to poor nations that wish to lift themselves by their bootstraps.

Food and Natural Resources

Writing in eighteenth-century England, Malthus saw famine, war, and pestilence as the inevitable deterrents to excessive population growth. Today, once more, there is grave question whether continued growth of world population will not outrun our food supply. As is true with most other great issues facing mankind, the more closely one examines the balance of food and population, the more difficult it is to come to an unequivocal conclusion. Long-term projections of food supplies are notoriously unreliable. We can only roughly estimate the current rate of growth of agricultural output.

[2] A. J. Coale, "The Economic Effects of Fertility Control in Underdeveloped Areas." In R. R. Green, Ed., *Human Fertility and Population Problems*, 1963.

Projections based on these estimates become increasingly
shaky if extended far into the future. Furthermore, one can
only speculate about the effect of changes in agricultural
technology and organization on future output. There may be
quantum jumps in technology deriving from artificial photo-
synthesis or from vastly improved methods of gathering food
from the sea.

Between 1934–1938 and 1961 it is estimated that there has
been a 14 per cent increase in world per capita grain production. But at the same time output of grain per person *decreased* 2 per cent in Asia and 16 per cent in Latin America. It
has risen 8 per cent in Africa and 5 per cent in Eastern Europe
and Russia, but the major progress has come in Australia–
New Zealand (up 51 per cent), North America (up 44 per
cent), and Western Europe (up 19 per cent). Global or
continental estimates of food deficits are based on fragmen-
tary data supplemented by more or less informed guesses.
They gloss over the very great differences in food production
and consumption from one country to another within a
continent and from one region to another within a country.
Nonetheless

. . . the accumulation of clinical evidence and medical judgment
supports the more recent studies based on food balance sheets
which indicate that in many countries millions of people get
insufficient calories and that there is an even wider and nutri-
tionally more serious shortage of proteins, minerals, and vitamins,
and probably of fats.[3]

India, with more than 450 million people, will have 187
million more in fifteen years. Thus in the next fifteen years
India will have to find a way of feeding an increase in

[3] G. R. Allen, "The World's Food Shortage: Nutritional Requirements and the Demand for Food." Paper presented at Iowa State
University Seminar, 1962.

population about equivalent to the present population of the United States. Since India has little additional land that can be brought into cultivation, her farmers must increase yields per acre on existing farm land by at least 50 per cent between now and 1980. A United States Department of Agriculture expert calculates that an additional 24 million tons of fertilizer a year must be applied to achieve this performance, but the entire world production of fertilizer is now only 28.6 million tons a year.[4]

It is entirely possible for India and most other countries in the world to grow or to import enough food at least to keep their people from starving in the next few decades. But this would require a revolution in traditional agricultural technology, as well as in arrangements of land tenure, credit, marketing, and transportation. The kinds of changes in attitudes and behavior that are likely to produce increased crop yields are analogous to those that would be required to bring down birth rates. India, in fact, is engaged in two large-scale, complementary efforts. One is a series of intensive experiments in which a "package" containing all elements required to improve agricultural productivity is applied to the land. The other is an intensive district program in family planning intended to apply the best technology and administration to a reduction in birth rates.

The future of the world's supply of raw materials other than food is also difficult to visualize with any certainty, but the situation is far from hopeless. The world's entire stock of fossil fuels (coal and oil) may be depleted in one hundred and fifty to two hundred years, but alternate energy resources, produced by atomic fission, possibly atomic fusion, and even by the sun,

[4] L. R. Brown, *Man, Land and Food—Looking Ahead at World Food Needs*. U. S. Department of Agriculture, 1963.

will probably mean that there will be sufficient energy for the world's use in the foreseeable future. It has been estimated that by the year 2000 10 to 20 per cent of energy consumption will be provided by electric generating plants powered by atomic energy.[5]

There will probably be enough iron, aluminum, and manganese to supply projected demands for the next forty years without significantly increasing costs, but there are likely to be shortages in copper, lead, and zinc. There are good substitutes for these metals, however, which will be used increasingly as the prices of the scarce metals rise. It is doubtful whether the world's forests will long be able to withstand the demands made upon them. But again it will be possible to substitute steel, aluminum, and other building materials for wood. Water demand and supply are exceedingly difficult to estimate far into the future. Assumptions must be made as to the extent of future investment in massive river development projects. The demineralization of brackish and even ocean water can be accomplished with existing technology and will become increasingly economic as inexpensive sources of energy, such as solar energy, are developed. But these optimistic predictions assume timely investment of huge amounts of capital to anticipate the demands of the growing population.

Burden of Dependency

Developing countries are kept poor by lack of productive capital (fertilizer and farm machinery, industrial plant and equipment) and by too few highly trained and motivated

[5] J. L. Fisher and N. Potter, "Resources in the United States and the World." In P. M. Hauser, Ed., *The Population Dilemma*, American Assembly, 1963.

technicians, engineers, and managers to make optimum use of that capital which is available. Capital accumulation is the essence of economic development. It is the primary path to increased income per capita. Aside from foreign economic aid and investment by foreigners, a nation accumulates capital by investing that part of its income not spent on consumption. In other words, the more a nation saves, the more is available for investment in productive capital.

In rich countries, which already have accumulated large amounts of capital, savings of individuals and business firms run between 10 and 20 per cent of national income. These savings are usually sufficient to provide as much new investment as is required by business and government. The problem in the developed countries is to maintain a level of investment high enough to absorb all the savings that individuals and business generate during periods of prosperity. On the other hand, in the capital-poor, developing world only a trickle of savings (from 0 to 7 per cent of national income) can be turned into productive capital.

The dramatic declines in mortality experienced in the developing countries have primarily affected infant and child mortality; they have not appreciably extended life expectancies at the upper end of the age scale. Thus, declining mortality, combined with relatively stable birth rates, has produced a "youngling" population, not an aging population. In the industrialized countries, the proportion of children under the age of fifteen is about 25 to 30 per cent; in the developing countries, children under fifteen constitute between 35 and 50 per cent of the population. These children—who are consumers for many years before they are producers—constitute a great burden of dependency that hinders economic development.

Countries with a rapidly growing population must spend a greater proportion of their income feeding their children, clothing and housing them, and providing them with a rudimentary education than is necessary in those nations in which population increases more slowly. With a given national income, a fast-growing population must spend so much on primary education to achieve minimum levels of literacy of its young children that it has little left over for the training of engineers; it must spend on family housing what it otherwise could invest in hydroelectric plants and steel mills.

In addition to its effect on the accumulation of capital, the dependency burden weighs heavily on the resources of a developing country that tries to provide its children with a minimum level of food, housing, and education. Those responsible for economic planning in Latin America, which has the world's fastest rate of population growth, and the emerging nations of Africa, even if there is no immediate problem of overcrowding, are overwhelmed by the amount of food, the numbers of new houses, schoolrooms, teachers, and slates and pencils that are implied by simple projections of population growth during the next decades.

Employment

With the passage of time the dependents in the zero to fifteen year age bracket will enter the fifteen to sixty-four age group, and look for work. It is obvious, but sometimes forgotten, that mere additions to the labor force do not necessarily mean that total production is increased. If the ratio of labor to productive capital is already high, as is the case in developing countries, more entrants to the labor force may mean more unemployment and underemployment. For example, in India it is estimated that 8 million new jobs were created from 1956–1961, but the working population increased by 10 million in the same period. As stated in the United Nations Report on the World Social Situation: [6]

. . . even if all the liberal provisions and estimates for the creation of additional employment that are contained in the various Asian development plans were to be completely fulfilled, the problem of rural unemployment and underemployment in most countries of the region will not be solved unless the efforts to control population growth prove more successful than they have in the past.

In the United States the postwar bumper crop of babies now becomes of age and enters the labor force at the time when technological advances require fewer, but more highly skilled, workers to achieve a given level of output. An intensified version of the same problem faces the developing country. Modern technology is directed toward producing more and more with less and less labor. With limited capital and an excess of labor, it would be logical to install new plant and equipment that maximizes the use of labor and minimizes the use of capital. But a country that desperately needs all the goods it can produce seeks the most "efficient" factories, and these do not use much labor. Furthermore, when a developing nation invests its scarce resources in a new steel mill or cement plant, it wants the latest model, not something that was obsolete in the West fifty years ago. Thus, in the developing world the very process of introducing and modernizing technology is likely to exacerbate the unemployment problem—at least in the short run. In any event, an increased number of unskilled laborers is hardly the key to economic development.

[6] *United Nations, Economic and Social Council Report on World Social Situation*, 1963.

Urbanization

The process of economic development has historically involved a movement of people from the countryside to the
cities in response to opportunities for gainful industrial employment. While large-scale urban migration takes place in
the developing countries, much of the mass movement to the
cities is not inspired by the call of employment but by the
desperate hope that some menial job or governmental relief
will be available there. Too often a man exchanges rural
underemployment for urban underemployment or unemployment. Kingsley Davis [7] estimates that if the population of
India increases as expected there will be between 100 and 200
million migrants to cities between 1960 and the end of this
century. In the year 2000 the largest city, Calcutta, will
contain between 36 and 66 million people. Calcutta, sprawl-
ing for hundreds of square miles, with a population of 66
million inadequately employed people, does not suggest ele-
vated levels of living. It suggests, instead, a concentration of
misery that can only have explosive consequences. The sheer
density of population under these circumstances presents
problems of the highest magnitude.

Waiting for the Demographic Transition

Despite the obstacles to capital accumulation presented by
population growth, the emerging countries are gradually becoming more industrialized, and great urban complexes are
rapidly growing. Some argue, therefore, that the developing
countries are bound to go through the demographic transition

[7] K. Davis, "Population." *Scientific American*, May 1963.

of late nineteenth-century Europe and the United States when a reduction in birth rates was a concomitant of increasing urbanization and industrialization. Thus, it is asserted that scarce resources and administrative effort would be more wisely applied to speed up the pace of industrial development than to finance national programs of fertility limitation.

With improvements in medicine and agriculture, and with economic well-being enhanced by technological and organizational advances in industry and commerce, mortality began to decline slowly in nineteenth-century Europe. Birth rates continued to average around 30 per 1,000 well into the century, but began to decline beginning about 1875 in Western Europe, and somewhat earlier in France. Despite some interesting demographic research on isolated vital statistics records, there is little comprehensive empirical data on which to construct an unassailable theory that accounts for the demographic transition. The introduction of the condom and diaphragm toward the end of the century is claimed to be an important influence, but there is evidence that *coitus interruptus*, practiced since antiquity, was, in fact, the most prevalent method of contraception. Kingsley Davis bases an explanation for the decline in birth rates on one of the most important forces that motivate human beings, "keeping up with the Joneses," or, as he identifies it in his presidential address before the Population Association of America,[8] the avoidance of "invidious deprivation." According to Davis, families strove to enhance their share of the new prosperity brought on by the industrial revolution (in Great Britain, for example, real per capita income in 1910–1914 was 2.3 times greater than in 1855–1859), and thus improve their social status relative to their neighbors. But declines in mortality

[8] K. Davis, "The Theory of Change and Response in Modern Demographic History." *Population Index*, October 1963.

meant that more children were living to share the family substance. Davis concludes:

. . . if each family is concerned with its prospective standing in comparison to other families within its reference group, we can understand why the peoples of the industrializing and hence prospering countries altered their demographic behavior in numerous ways to have the effect of reducing the population growth brought about by lowered mortality.

There are, however, profound differences between the situation that prevails today in the developing countries and the circumstances under which the industrialized Western nations, followed by Japan, underwent their demographic transition. The surge in population brought about by swift declines in mortality through imported public health measures is taking place at an earlier stage of development than was the case in the West. Davis [9] points out that in Great Britain "the peak of human multiplication came when the country was already highly industrialized and urbanized with only one-fifth of its working males in agriculture," while declines in fertility did not occur until much later. If European patterns are retraced, it may take the developing countries at least thirty to sixty years to arrive at a state of industrialization that will bring with it declines in fertility. But in the meantime, population is growing much more swiftly than ever before in history. The rate of natural increase (births minus deaths) rarely rose above 1.5 per cent in nineteenth-century Europe, but between 1950 and 1960 it averaged 3.2 per cent per year in Taiwan, 2.7 per cent in Ceylon, 3.2 in Malaya, and 3.4 in El Salvador.[10]

[9] "Population." *Scientific American*, May 1963.
[10] *Cf.* K. Davis, "The Theory of Change and Response in Modern Demographic History," *op. cit.*

With rates such as these per capita income is more likely to fall than to rise during the coming decades. The growth in prosperity that Davis sees as a condition precedent to fertility reduction in the face of declining mortality is not likely to be achieved by the masses in the developing countries. When poverty is all-pervasive, one child more or less does not seem to make much difference, particularly if he is part of an extended family in which brothers, and even first cousins and their families, live under one roof, pool their property and earnings, and share responsibility for rearing the young. On the other hand, the urbanized, prosperous elite almost universally take the lead in limiting the size of their families. Unfortunately, they constitute only the thinnest layer of population in these countries. Unless their example influences the behavior of the people at large, their action will have little effect on national birth rates.

Economics of Fertility Limitation

One cannot escape the conclusion that it is wishful thinking to expect the forces of industrialization and urbanization to bring down birth rates in the developing countries within the next few decades without deliberate action. Government officials sometimes talk about levying a tax that rises progressively with the number of children in a family, or removing the subsidy that is awarded in some countries on the basis of family size. But this would be inhumane as well as politically suicidal. A much more attractive measure politically would be the establishment of a social security scheme under which parents would no longer feel the need for many children as old-age insurance. But developing countries are criticized for devoting too much of their limited substance to welfare benefits; they could ill afford a really effective social security system.

The dollar-and-cents benefits derived from a reduction in the birth rate are so great that governments are justified in allocating a substantial share of national resources to programs of fertility limitation, provided, of course, the programs are effective. Economists who have attempted estimates conclude that a dollar invested in fertility control is many times as effective in increasing income per capita as a dollar invested in plant and equipment. One economist calculates that for India the present value of a representative newborn baby's lifetime consumption is $200 whereas the present value of his lifetime future production is about $75. He concludes that the government can afford to pay $125 for each birth prevented.[11] But there still remains the much more uncertain determination of the number of births prevented per dollar of expenditure on a given family planning program. Dr. Berelson's review of fertility limitation programs now in progress will give us some indications as to the effectiveness of these programs. But those who are responsible for the direction of economic and social development of their nations must do the best job they can with the knowledge available to calculate the costs—in political, social, and ethical terms, as well as in rupees or pesos—of national programs of fertility limitation and to balance these costs against the political, social, ethical, and monetary costs of letting the growth of population take its natural course.

[11] S. Enke, "The Economics of Government Payments to Limit Population." *Economic Development and Cultural Change*, July 1960, pp. 339–48.

Family Planning Programs Throughout the World

Bernard Berelson

The problem is given: undue population growth threatens the socioeconomic development of countries with two-thirds of the world's people. As we all know, the death rate has been sharply lowered in many of the developing countries since World War II, so that they and the world now have the largest growth rates in all of human history. Death control will not be passed by once available, and emigration is clearly no answer. Thus something must be done about birth rates if population growth is to be controlled in the interests of national development.

Beyond that utilitarian objective, historically important as it is, lies another consideration that deserves mention. So much dramatic attention has been given to the striking numbers of the population problem that it is too often seen as simply a matter of quantities. Nothing could be more misleading: what is at stake is the very quality of life as indicated not only by economic prosperity but by democratic political institutions, educational opportunities, personal health, and the effective freedom of people everywhere to determine family size in line with their own desires and consciences, as we do in this privileged country.

Birth rates can be lowered in one of three ways: by late marriage and not marrying, as in Ireland; by induced abortion, as in Japan and the Eastern European countries; or by contraception, as in all the Western countries. As for the marriage practices of a society, they are closely bound up with its social and cultural institutions, and hence are not easily or quickly changed. Induced abortion is widely and legally practiced in some countries—Japan and some Eastern European countries maintain low birth rates through its use—and it is quite widely but illegally and badly practiced in many others. It is, however, unacceptable to most societies on religious or moral grounds. Indeed, the very fact of widespread abortion is itself sometimes used as an important argument for voluntary fertility regulation as, for example, in Latin America today.

The most successful means of fertility regulation, then, appears to be contraception. In the remainder of my remarks I shall deal primarily with this road to the limitation of population growth. But it is by no means a narrow road: the voluntary control of births by the individual couple is so close to the heart of life that there is scarcely an important element in human behavior that is not involved—cultural institutions, religious beliefs, economic arrangements, family organization, sexual practices. In consequence, it is noteworthy that the norm of the small family and the practice of family limitation have been established across a wide range of societies: across religious affiliations, as in Catholic southern Europe and Protestant northern Europe; across political ideologics, as with the United States and the Soviet bloc; across industrial and agricultural economies, rich and poor nations, better-educated and poorer-educated societies, as within Europe; across the West and the East, as with Japan; and, perhaps just beginning, across the tropical countries as well as the temperate ones.

Up to the last few years the headline on population has

been: There Is a Problem! Now that headline may be changing. For the first time in the history of the world, through
deliberate and governmentally approved action, something is
being done, and it begins to appear that something can indeed
be done. Let us review what is now going on in this field.

To begin with, there are now five countries with official
governmentally approved and administered programs to implement family planning: India, Pakistan, South Korea, Tunisia, and Turkey (and probably mainland China as well). India
was the first country to adopt a national policy of limiting
population and, subject to lack of firm knowledge about
mainland China, it is the largest country to be working on this
problem. India set up Family Planning Boards in the mid-
1950s, both in the National Health Ministry and in the states.
At the outset, and for some period thereafter, the program
consisted of the clinical approach, but it slowly became clear
that an extensive community-aimed effort would be needed to
take the program to the people rather than expecting them to
come to it. In the last few years the family planning agency in
India has concentrated on setting up the administrative machinery to carry a program to the people by assigning a
medical family planning officer and supporting staff at the
district level (1 to 2 million population) and organizing a
small educational and field staff at the block level (70,000–
100,000 population). The present governmental budget for
family planning is more than $5,000,000 a year, or about one
cent per capita, but plans for the next five years call for
substantially increased expenditures.

A similar picture can be presented for the other large
country with an official national program, India's neighbor
Pakistan. A national program was set up in 1960—in effect
two programs, because of the organization of the country into

two wings, geographically separated. The annual budget is also
just over one cent per capita, or about 8 per cent of the total
budget for health. The family planning program to date has
consisted of a series of short training courses for medical and
para-medical personnel, the addition of family planning services to 1,600 medical units throughout the country, the establishment of a national Research Institute of Family Planning,
limited clinical studies of the new methods of contraception,
small-scale experimentation with mobile audio-visual vans in
areas where there are no medical centers, limited use of the
mass media, and three major research studies to provide
guidance for the program. Progress is slow, but gradually the
institutions and personnel to carry forward a national program
are being developed; and the plans for the Third Five-Year
Plan, to begin next year, call for a much enlarged budget and
an upgrading of positions and personnel. In addition, the
newly appointed commissioner of family planning is actively
seeking ways to develop an intensive program in Pakistan
centered on the newly-developed intra-uterine contraceptive
device (IUD), which promises to be extremely important in
all the developing countries.

Both India and Pakistan, of course, have very large populations—the second and fifth or sixth largest in the world—and
it is partly their size that has held back the progress desired
and often anticipated. The third Asian country to organize an
official national program, South Korea, is much smaller—
about 28 to 30 million—and at the moment more successful in
spreading family planning. Here the government has given a
high priority to family planning, both in national budget
(about 4.5 cents per capita) and in call upon other resources.
Three full-time family planning workers, nurse-midwives, are
employed in every one of the country's 180 health centers. In

addition, 1,400 assistant workers have been recruited from village women with elementary education, or one for each subdistrict of 10 to 20,000 population. In the summer of 1964 a special IUD effort was made, and it already appears that this method is highly popular: insertions now number about 60,-000 (more than anywhere in the world) and, for the time being, seem limited only by available medical personnel and governmental subsidies. In my own view, Korea is one of the two or three countries with the best chance to demonstrate for the first time in human history that a deliberate effort to spread voluntary contraception can bring down a national birth rate in a reasonably short period of time.

Tunisia embarked upon this effort only this year, and the program is just getting under way. Already, however, it appears that the demand for family planning is greater than the resources available to satisfy it, but training and organizational work will soon repair the balance. So far, in both Korea and Tunisia the program has dealt exclusively with voluntary contraception, but it is appropriate to report that in both countries the Ministry of Justice has been instructed to study liberalizing the law governing induced abortion. While it is too early to say what will result from such study, I cite this development as an indication of how seriously the highest governmental officers view the population problem that confronts them.

Finally, in Turkey family planning has been given a prominent place in the current officially-approved plan for economic development, a program has been laid out, a director of family planning appointed, a budget accepted, a fertility survey completed, a private family planning association formed—and intensive action awaits only the repeal of an anti-contraception law dating from the difficult days that faced

Turkey after World War I. Once that law is off the books, the favorable factors are such that here, too, one might expect a highly successful effort in a relatively short time.

In all these countries, I might add, technical assistance has been provided by American private foundations, notably The Ford Foundation and The Population Council. Expert missions have drawn up reports and plans for each of these countries, and American specialists are resident advisors in each of them at this moment.

Those countries have official policies, but there are a number of others that are implementing family planning with governmental support in funds and facilities but without an official declaration. Most notable in this category, perhaps, is Taiwan, another leading contender for the historical distinction of success in voluntary population control. After a highly successful effort in Taichung, a city of 350,000 population, the health officials expanded the program last spring to about 10 per cent of the island's population in the more deprived rural and urban areas. Already, after only a matter of months, that program is being expanded again to the entire island of 12,000,000 population. There is careful documentation that the Taichung program brought down the birth rate in that city and there is every indication that the island-wide program will be similarly successful. Here, again, as in Korea, the program is centered on the newly-developed intra-uterine device. And a similar concentration on the IUD is being expedited in Hong Kong through governmental support to the private family planning association, again with more clients than can currently be served.

Nor is that all. In several other countries limited projects are going forward under governmental auspices—as in Ceylon, where the Swedish government is providing technical assistance; or in Thailand, where the first fertility survey of knowledge about family planning, attitudes toward it, and actual contraceptive practice has just been completed with American help, and where the first action program will get under way this year (and, to illustrate the international character of this movement, advised by the Taiwanese doctor who supervised the Taichung program and who is being sent to Bangkok by an American foundation); or in Egypt, where a few clinics are offering family planning services under governmental auspices; or in Indonesia, Fiji, Malaysia, Chile, Venezuela, Jamaica, Puerto Rico, Nigeria, Ghana, and Southern Rhodesia, where IUD programs are being undertaken in various medical installations.

In several of these countries there have been carefully controlled and scientifically measured experiments to determine whether family planning could be implemented, and if so how that can be done most efficiently (with, incidentally, a few such studies in our own country). It would be too much to claim that they were all successful, but it is fair, I think, to say that we have learned from all of them. Moreover, a number of so-called fertility surveys have been carried on over the past few years; therefore we now have a good start toward more or less comparable data on knowledge, attitude, and practice from a large number of countries throughout the world— Argentina, Brazil, Ceylon, Chile, Costa Rica, Czechoslovakia, Egypt, Ghana, Greece, Hungary, India, Indonesia, Israel, Italy, Jamaica, Japan, Korea, Lebanon, Mexico, Pakistan, Peru, Puerto Rico, San Salvador, Taiwan, Tunisia, Turkey, Uruguay, the United Kingdom, the United States, and Venezuela. To my best knowledge this is the most substantial set of comparative social data ever collected across such a range of societies, and a few of the pilot projects in family planning are among the most elaborate and extensive social experiments ever carried out in the natural setting.

Thus throughout the world, on every continent, involving every race and every religion, the problems presented by population pressures are increasingly being recognized. Slowly, often tentatively, sometimes reluctantly, but still surely, impelled by the pressures and encouraged by the favorable response of the people themselves, countries are moving from the problem toward a program.

What has been learned from all this experience to guide the continuing effort? In order to keep in good standing with my research colleagues, I must remark that everything is always more complicated than my quick review will suggest, and that others would summarize the experience differently, but to my mind there are several conclusions that are justified by developments to date. Here are just a few of them:

The straight clinical approach to the spread of family planning does not work well. A much more active program of taking family planning to the people is required.

Substantial proportions of the people want family planning now; contrary to the usual belief, sufficient motivation exists to make a demographic difference if it could be implemented. To be sure, the actual practice of family planning is minimal in the typical developing country, and knowledge about contraception and reproductive physiology is not much better. With regard to attitudes toward family planning, however, the situation is different. Virtually every survey on attitudes toward family planning, from urban America to village India, shows that a large proportion of people say they are favorable to the idea of limiting family size, and especially after the third or fourth child. The figures vary somewhat from one locality to another, but there is an impressive body of favorable responses from India and Pakistan, from Mexico and Peru, from Jamaica and Puerto Rico, from Thailand and Turkey, from the United States and Great Britain. Many people in the world are now persuaded, at least in principle, of the desirability of limiting the birth of children to the number wanted when they are wanted—and everywhere that means fewer than they now have. Thus, if all couples throughout the world were equally able to realize their own desires on number and timing of children, if unwanted children were not born, a great measure of the population problem would disappear.

The "ready" people are likely to be of two kinds: those of high socioeconomic status, and particularly high education; and those of high parity, particularly those with three children or more, including sons. Almost by definition there are too few of the former for a sizable effect on the birth rate anywhere in the developing countries, but there are many of the latter. Studies like that in Taiwan are beginning to show that highly educated people will undertake family planning on their own and in the absence of any organized program, but that a program will be able to reach those of high parity.

The character of the contraceptive technology makes a very big difference. Anything that can overcome the need for sustained motivation, repetitive action, and a system for continued supplies is a big step forward. Moreover, the easier and more effective the method, the less the motivation needed to achieve successful family planning. Hence the intra-uterine device is a great advance.

The indicated strategy for spreading family planning, under most conditions, is to aim at skimming the cream of motivated people on the double ground that that will yield the most return per unit of scarce resources and that the best way to spread motivation is to satisfy the existing motivation.

Again, studies like Taiwan are showing that word-of-mouth diffusion can be very effective, at least with the new intrauterine device. A corollary is that action programs should begin in the cities and towns and then move out more or less concentrically from them.

As for cost, it begins to appear that family planning can be implemented economically—that is, for far less than the strictly economic value of each prevented birth. Family planning has many more values than the economic one, and perhaps more important ones—social, educational, cultural, political, and personal values—but in narrowly economic terms it is clearly justified and almost certainly worth while. Indeed, for many developing countries it may be the best investment they can make.

I do not wish to leave the impression that it is an easy task to bring effective family planning to the population of a developing country—to a population characterized by universal marriage, early marriage, subordinate women, high infant mortality, illiteracy, the desire for sons to secure one's old age, ignorance of the means and consequences of family planning, sparse medical and administrative resources, lack of commercial channels for distributing supplies, traditional political and moral objections, general poverty. In the national and pilot programs under way so far there have inevitably been mistakes, false starts, disappointments, and frustrations—in short, it sometimes seems, nearly as many errors as trials. Some people take such critical observations and occasional failures as demonstrating the impossibility of doing anything effective about the matter.

But how could it be otherwise on such a problem? Has deliberate effort ever done any better, or as well, on a matter of this scope and character? In less than a decade we have developed a layer of experience, a solid body of knowledge, a number of trained personnel, an improved technology, and a plan of strategic attack to deal with one of the most important problems in the world. Yet we are still near the beginning. And, to this date, for various local reasons, we have nowhere in the world yet witnessed a maximum effort in this field—an effort, that is, truly commensurate with the problem. The consequences for mankind can be great—in international amity, in national development, in family welfare, in standard of living, in freedom, in quality of life. Under the circumstances, the accomplishments to date seem to me to be an occasion for pride, not disappointment, for hope, not despair, and, looking to the next decade, for great expectations.

United States and United Nations
Population Policy

Richard N. Gardner

From the perspective of one who tries, however imperfectly, to serve his country from a desk in the Department of State concerned with international organizational affairs, I want first to review very quickly the implications of population trends for the kind of world we seek; second, to describe in just a thumbnail sketch some of the recent trends in thinking in our country and the evolution of the American debate, and, I hope, the growth of consensus in this area; third, to capture for you, if I may try to do so, the great debate which took place in the United Nations on this two years ago and forecast perhaps a little what could happen this year; and, finally, in a very tentative—and frankly apologetic, because it will be inadequate—way, to suggest some guidelines for American policy in the future.

On the first issue, that is, the implications of all this for the kind of world we seek, I shall say very little because there are better qualified people to spell out for you in fine detail the meaning of these awesome statistics. I will just say this: Until very recently Western thought was characterized by an optimistic faith in the inevitability of progress. Things were expected to get better and better every year. And, despite two terrible wars, a great depression, and revolutionary ferment that is shaking our civilization to its very foundations, people have still clung to this belief as time has gone on. But it is getting harder and harder to be sure of this, and one of the reasons is the demographic explosion. Because, despite all the progress of science and technology in recent years, there are more people living in misery and deprivation in the world today than there were at the turn of the century. Of course there are also more people enjoying adequate living standards. But the increase in the number of underprivileged has been far greater than the increase in those who are in adequate circumstances.

Whether such a development can be called progress is, to say the least, a highly questionable fact. Now, I know there are people who like to cite the charts showing that the gross national product or gross national something is going up and up and up, but we know that the test of progress is the realization of the potentialities of the individual human being. Man does not live by bread alone. You cannot measure progress in active statistics. You cannot even measure progress in per capita income. I suggest, for quite obvious reasons, that the unchecked growth in fertility perils gravely the realization of those political, economic, cultural, and spiritual aims which should be common to all the great religious faiths. Now I just state this as a matter of personal belief, and I go on to say that if the condition of the individual, and not gross statistics, is to be the measure of progress, then it is absolutely essential that we be concerned about population trends.

As long as we are concerned with the quality of life, we must be concerned with the quantity of life. Now there are some people who say, "There is no real problem about population because agricultural productivity is growing, industrial productivity is growing, there is lots of room, so we won't face a problem for one hundred years, two hundred years." But this is a static and not dynamic analysis and, if I may say so, it is not adequately grounded in the scientific evidence. It is at best a half truth because we have to face the fact that in the world today more than two-thirds of humanity are living in totally unacceptable circumstances, and the only hope they have of raising their living standards is to accumulate capital which can be invested in productive enterprise and in social capital. And if population growth is so fast that it eats up every increase in national income, there can be no surplus capital to invest.

Just to dramatize this with a few figures: the United Nations has set as a growth goal for the United Nations' decade of development, which is this decade, an average increase in national income in the less developed two-thirds of humanity of 5 per cent a year. That is not very much because we are talking about an average per capita income, per person income, in these countries of about $70 to $100 a year. That means these people earn per day about what you or I would spend when we go to the drugstore to buy a pack of cigarettes. That is about the living standard on about $70 to $100 per year. And the United Nations' target, as I say, is very modest—5 per cent increase a year which would mean that a $100 country would be $200 per capita in a generation. It would be, that is, if the population were stable, but in many of these countries the population is growing at 3 per cent a year, so even if they achieved a 5 per cent growth in national income, you subtract a 3 per cent annual growth in population and you are left with a 2 per cent increase in individual living standards, and that is not much.

Now there is obviously much that we do not know about the relationship of population growth to economic and social development. But I must say I am satisfied, from looking at the economic evidence, with this conclusion: that existing rates of population growth in certain less developed countries make it virtually impossible at the present time, even with the maximum of foreign aid and the maximum of internal sacrifice, to bring about a rate of economic growth that will provide the rate of improvement in individual living standards that these countries seek to attain and which, more fundamentally, is vital to the proper exercise of the individual's human faculties.

Now let me make one thing clear before I leave this introductory subject. Family planning and the limitation of population increases are not a cure-all. They are not a substitute for foreign aid. Unfortunately, population growth in the future is predetermined to a large extent by the population growth of the past. Thanks to the rapid increase of recent years, children under fifteen years of age account for about 40 per cent of total population in less developed countries. When this group passes through the childbearing years, population increase will be very substantial even if family size falls. Moreover, further reductions in mortality rates can be expected as the benefits of modern science and technology are brought increasingly to the developing nations. And for these reasons and because appropriate measures to reduce the birth rate in different countries may take time to discover and carry out, it may be many, many years before significant reductions take place in rates of population growth. And even if growth rates fall, we shall have to learn to live during this century, at least, with continuous large increases in world population.

To sum it up in a very rough way, I would doubt that any acceptable measure of family planning that can be found will prevent the world population by the year 2000 from growing from the present 3 billion to at least 5 billion. The projection is between 6 and 7 billion. If effective measures were started around the world now one might bring that down, but it is going to be nearly double in the year 2000 what it is today.

The population problem should, therefore, not be regarded as the only problem. We still need a foreign-aid program, we still need effective measures of trade, we still need to work for human dignity in many other areas. So it is not the answer, but it is, I would venture to say to you, the *sine qua non*. Measures to deal with the population problem can be no substitute for economic assistance, but what is done in the next few years about the population problem can make the difference between rates of population growth that are compatible with substantial material progress and human dignity, and those rates of growth that spell certain misery for the majority of the world's people. That is the issue.

Let me turn now to the second element of my theme—the United States position. All of you know that there has been a major change in opinion in this country in recent years about this problem. I think it is a truly extraordinary, and I would venture to say from my point of view constructive, change. This is a subject which can now be discussed, can be discussed seriously. And the fact that meetings of this kind have been held in the last several years is the most eloquent testimony to this fact. Distinguished leaders of our society have begun to speak out on this question. President Kennedy, about a year before his tragic death, said in response to a press conference question that we need to "know more about the whole reproductive cycle and this knowledge should then be made available to the world." The Department of State and the Agency for International Development have distributed to embassies and aid missions around the world an official policy statement made in the United Nations, declaring that the United States would "help other countries, upon request, to find potential sources of information and assistance on ways and means of dealing with these population problems." The United States Government at the World Health Assembly in Geneva called for more World Health Organization research in the medical aspects of human reproduction and pledged $500,000 to this end. The Congress adopted an amendment to the Foreign Aid Bill by Senator Fulbright, authorizing the use of foreign and development research funds "to conduct research into the problems of population growth." Two distinguished senators, Joseph Clark of Pennsylvania and Ernest Gruening of Alaska, introduced a joint resolution requesting the President of the United States "speedily to implement the policies of the United States regarding population growth as declared before the United Nations by inaugurating substantially increased programs of research within the national institutes of health and by taking steps to make the results of such research freely available to countries requesting such assistance." Former President Dwight D. Eisenhower, who had stated as President, in 1959, that "I cannot imagine anything more emphatically a subject that is not a proper political or governmental activity or function or responsibility," now declared: "As I now look back, it may be that I was carrying that conviction too far . . . we should tell receiving nations how population growth threatens them and what can be done about it." And, of course, Dr. John Rock attracted national attention with his book, *The Time Has Come*, in which he called for an end to controversy and for further research to find family-planning techniques acceptable to all religious groups.

I will not go on detailing these developments. They do reveal, I think, a growing consensus that there is a serious problem here which affects the future of our society and of human freedom in the world, a problem which deserves to be at the forefront of public discussion and a problem on which solutions acceptable to all may well be emerging before we know it.

About the same time that this debate was gathering force in our country, the first debate on this subject in the history of the United Nations took place. It was an extraordinary experience for those of us who took part in it. I know there are those who denigrate the United Nations as a debating society, but what a debating society it is! What better forum to air the views of all the countries about great issues of our time? Here was an opportunity for every country to state its views on the subject, and I dare say we Americans learned more about the attitudes of other countries in this debate than perhaps in any other comparable event of recent years. I cannot possibly do justice to this great discussion in a brief paper. I will just say this: There were four principal viewpoints put forward in this debate, and I take the liberty of summarizing them because it is very important to have an overview of what the world thinks of this problem.

One school of thought in the United Nations was represented by the government of Sweden and certain other co-sponsors of a resolution which was laid on the table at the United Nations—countries like Ceylon, Denmark, Ghana, Greece, Nepal, Norway, Pakistan—which represented a wide variety of different regions of the world. These nations argued that population growth posed grave problems for economic and social development, and that urgent action must be taken to cope with it. They urged a major increase in United Nations activity in the population field—including technical assistance in the field of family planning.

Another viewpoint was advanced on the other side of the spectrum by Argentina and Ireland, with support from some other countries, principally in Latin America. These countries questioned the existence of a population problem. They challenged the right of the United Nations to discuss it, and they were particularly outspoken in opposing a United Nations program in family planning financed from technical assistance funds to which they were contributing.

A third viewpoint, somewhere between these extremes, was expressed by a substantial number of member states, including France and other countries of continental Europe, some French-African states, and some Latin-American countries. This group conceded the existence of population problems in some areas but argued that action by the United Nations should be deferred pending further study. They opposed the granting of technical assistance by the United Nations and proposed instead an inquiry to find out exactly what precise kinds of assistance were required by member countries.

A fourth and very strange viewpoint was expressed by the members of the Soviet bloc. During the General Assembly debate, the Soviet Union and some of the Eastern European countries expounded the traditional communist position that Western discussions of the population problem were based on what they called "neo-Malthusian fallacies," and, of course, they said population problems ceased to exist under communism. As one may suppose, this communist line was poorly received by the members of the United Nations. At least one very courageous representative of a less developed country chided the Russians for favoring planning in all sectors of economic life except the human sector—the one most important in its implications for economic and social growth.

One may ask what about the United States—where did it

stand? We made a strong statement underlining the importance of the population problem in terms of the purposes of the United Nations and world peace. We urged the need for more knowledge about it, the necessity for each country to determine its own population policy in accordance with its own economic, social, and religious circumstances, and the willingness of the United States to help other countries upon request to find potential sources of information and assistance on ways and means of dealing with the population problem. When it came to a vote on the controversial technical assistance paragraph, the United States abstained for a number of reasons I would like to set out here. We abstained, first, because we thought this technical assistance provision was superfluous, neither adding to nor subtracting from the authority already possessed by the United Nations to grant technical assistance upon request to a member nation. Second, and this is most important, because it was not clear from the debate whether technical assistance would involve the actual supply of contraceptive devices, which the United States would not have supported and did not support. And third, because in the light of the differences of opinion among member states expressed during the debate, it seemed best to us for the immediate future to emphasize the three areas in which there appeared to be a broad consensus, namely, information, training, and discussion of the population problem.

Let me now turn very briefly to the future. Where do we go from here? I have briefly recounted the debate in the United Nations. I have referred to the growing consensus in our own country. I suggest that a large measure of common ground is emerging. To begin with, the desire for increased knowledge about population trends is now nearly universal. We have passed almost without noticing it from a period in which the great uncertainty concerned the existence of a world population problem to a period in which the great uncertainty is what can and should be done about it. Moreover, even in the matter of what should be done about it, there is now, I may venture to suggest, no significant body of responsible opinion among people of any major religious, ethical, or ideological persuasion that advocates totally unplanned or unregulated fertility, although there are sincere differences of opinion about the means that are morally permissible and the effectiveness of the means that are available.

There is, I believe, virtually universal agreement on both ethical and practical grounds, that decisions about responsible parenthood can be made only by individual parents themselves in the light of their responsibilities to their children and their society, and to the moral values which govern alike parents, children, and societies. Now what we in the United States Government are trying to do is to develop out of this merging consensus a blueprint for international cooperation. It will have four main elements.

The first is to encourage more information and analysis of demographic problems. We have got to know what the problem is. Responsible policy makers in less developed countries have to know what their populations are, what the growth rates are, what the composition of the population is, what are the implications of these trends for their aspirations for their people. And in this great effort of information and analysis, the United Nations, as an objective international authority with no ax to grind, can play a very important role.

The second area is medical research. We believe there should be a great increase in research efforts both within our country and through international agencies to deal with the question, to help us find acceptable methods of family planning which can be utilized in different areas of the world.

The third facet of our blueprint is the development in the less developed countries of an adequate network of health and social services, because no family planning program can be carried out in a primitive society whose people are largely illiterate, where there are no doctors, no nurses, no auxiliary personnel, and the people are living in total impoverishment without any motivation. Education and the development of an infrastructure of health and social services are obviously needed.

Fourth and last, of course, is the sensitive one, the actual implementation of family planning programs. This is the only major area in which disagreements exist and may continue to exist for some time. We believe that countries seeking help in the implementation of family planning programs should have access to the wide variety of sources of assistance available throughout the world.

The Agency for International Development is in a position to refer requests for medical assistance in family planning to appropriate agencies of the United States Government, such as the Public Health Service, to private organizations, to universities, and to foundations. It does not, however, use government funds for the shipment of manufactured contraceptives. The provision of these materials can readily be made by those governments whose citizens are not divided on this question and by private foundations. And for similar reasons United Nations activity, in our judgment, should concentrate on training and the supply of information, and stop short of providing the actual birth-control materials.

In conclusion, I offer this one final thought: Much has already been accomplished in arousing the world's concern with the population problem. The further challenge now for all of us is to devise programs of action founded on the principle of free choice, programs that make sense in political as well as in technical terms. In meeting this challenge, our fundamental concern should be to get the job done, not to draw unnecessary doctrinal issues.

Ambassador Adlai Stevenson put it very well a year ago. He said:

In this field, marked by deep differences of conviction, by slogans, by emotion, it may be possible for statesmen to discern underlying principles not fully apparent to the intense partisan. In this field we need not fear differences of conviction. In this field, so intimately intertwined with the most basic facts of human life and existence, we *must* fear ignorance, inattention, easy and facile solutions.

We know, only too well, that there is no one, simple solution to this many-faceted problem. And even with respect to the most important aspect, responsible parenthood, the obstacle is not the intransigence of one group or another.

The obstacle is not political timidity; it is not lack of concensus. The true obstacle is the long neglect of population problems, only now beginning to be remedied by scientists, by theologians, by administrators, by social scientists, and by statesmen.

This long neglect is now on the way to being remedied. That is the principal meaning of the great debates which have recently taken place in the United States and the United Nations.

ATTITUDES OF OUR SOCIETY TO THE POPULATION QUESTION

WILLIAM E. MORAN, JR.

This paper attempts a brief portrait of the attitudes of our society toward the question of the world's rapid population growth and the way in which such growth may be a threat to stability and peace. Such a presentation should help interested and responsible Catholics to understand how their fellows in this country and elsewhere feel about this problem. It is appropriate and timely to take such a survey because there has been a very substantial change over the last few years in the way in which our society has come to see this problem. When I speak of our society, I mean primarily, but not exclusively, our fellow Americans. We are, of course, a part of a broader international society, and what our fellows abroad think has an impact on our own thinking and must be taken into account.

In this portrayal I shall consider the changes in our public policy, public discussions of the subject, its treatment in the mass media, and the action programs of our government and of international agencies. This should at least illustrate what areas of our society are concerned with rapid population growth, how they see such growth presenting a problem, and what they think should be done about it.

Changes in Public Policy

Let me cite two of what may well be the more significant indications of how, in the public sector, attitudes have rapidly changed over the last four or five years. In 1959 General William H. Draper issued a report of a President's Committee to study the United States Military Assistance Programs. This report suggested that foreign aid would have to be accompanied by birth control if the good effects of the aid were not to be nullified by excessive population growth. It proposed that the United States furnish birth-control information on request to other countries. In December 1959, however, President Eisenhower said, "I cannot imagine anything more emphatically a subject that is not a proper political or governmental action or function or responsibility . . . we do not intend to interfere with the internal affairs of any other government and if they want to do something . . . about what is admittedly a very difficult question, an almost explosive question, that is their business. And if they want to go to someone for help, they should go, they will go unquestionably to professional groups not to governments. This government will not . . . as long as I am here, have a positive political document in its program that has to do with this problem of birth control. That's not our business."

In December 1962 Dr. Richard N. Gardner, Deputy Assistant Secretary of the Department of State for International Organization Affairs, speaking for the United States in the United Nations, said it would "help other countries, upon request, to find potential sources of information and assistance on ways and means of dealing with population problems."

In 1963 President Kennedy, in response to a press conference question, declared that we need to "know more about the whole reproductive cycle" and that this knowledge should then "be made more available to the world." Following this up, the National Academy of Sciences in a brochure entitled *The Growth of World Population*, dated April 17, 1963, recommended that substantial increases should be made in research for better understanding of the physiology and bio-chemistry of the reproductive process and, for pilot projects, for developing new, basic knowledge in new techniques, procedures, devices, and medically active compounds for the regulation of fertility.

In the fall of 1963 former President Eisenhower stated: "When I was president, I opposed the use of federal funds to provide birth-control information to countries we were aiding because I felt this would violate the deepest religious convictions of large groups of taxpayers. As I now look back, it may be that I was carrying that conviction too far. I still believe that as a national policy we should not make birth-control programs a condition to our foreign aid, but we should tell receiving nations how population growth threatens them and what can be done about it. Also, it seems quite possible that scientific research, if mobilized for the purpose, could develop new biological knowledge which would enable nations to hold their human fertility to nonexplosive levels without violating any moral or religious precepts."

The Agency for International Development now provides information and consultants for family planning programs. This is an extension of its long-term practice of providing assistance in the field of census taking and demography. The Agency does not as yet provide financial assistance for the procurement of materials or the building of facilities to produce them.

In November 1959 the Catholic bishops of the United

States, meeting in Washington, had reacted quite adversely to the Draper Report. In 1960 Norman St. John-Stevas prepared a report to the Center for the Study of Democratic Institutions on Birth Control and Public Policy as a part of a comprehensive study of morals and law in connection with the Center's study of religious institutions. This has now been reprinted under the title *Birth Control and Public Policy* by the Family Life Bureau of the National Catholic Welfare Conference. The following statement from his introduction is worthy of thoughtful consideration: "It is most unlikely that Americans will ever reach ultimate agreement on the morality of birth control. Conceivably, though, some working agreement about public policy can be achieved. That agreement will not be reached in an atmosphere clogged with exaggerated charges, emotional recriminations, and sloganeering. It will require a cool knowledge of the factual situation, of the arguments made for and against the disputed practice, and of the proper relationship between morals and the law." His study is completed with twenty-three concisely stated conclusions, of which the following three are especially pertinent here:

20). World population growth presents a challenge to the Christian conscience to secure an intense and concerted international effort to raise living standards. Given such an effort, the prospects for a very considerable increase in world food production are favorable.

22). Receipt of help under the United States foreign-aid program should not be made conditional on the adoption of artificial birth-control policies by the recipient state, nor should foreign-aid funds be used to implement such programs, even at the request of the designated state.

23). The United Nations' policy of neutrality on the question of contraception is the only one possible in view of the conflicting opinions of member states. Rhythm is the only method of birth control that would be acceptable as a means of international family planning.

The first of these conclusions recognizes the challenge presented by rapid population growth in the world and is cited for that reason. The last two are cited to show how things have changed since 1960. In this scholarly study these two positions were altogether reasonable when written. What has happened to the first of them can be seen in the change in American policy noted above. The second reflected the fact that a great many Catholic countries represented in the United Nations refused to agree that the United Nations had any right to deal with the question of population limitation.

On December 18, 1962, however, the United Nations General Assembly concluded the first debate in its history, devoted entirely to the subject of population. It adopted by sixty-nine affirmative votes (including that of the United States), twenty-seven abstentions, and not a single negative vote, a major resolution calling for an intensified population program through international cooperation. The Latin-American countries had come to a decisive change in their attitudes. The Catholic negative bloc had been broken. There was still no agreement that the United Nations should have an action program aimed at population limitation—but this question will be considered in the next General Assembly.

From the 10th to the 20th of December 1963 there was held in New Delhi the first Asian population conference jointly sponsored by the United Nations Economic Commission for Asia and the Far East, the Bureau of Social Affairs, and the Bureau of Technical Assistance Operations in cooperation with the government of India. (It should be noted in passing that a number of Catholics from Japan, the Philippines, and India participated effectively in this conference.) Now the

United Nations is making preparations for a world population conference to be held in 1965 in Belgrade. Thus in the few short years since 1960 we moved from the position where a most perceptive observer felt "the United Nations' policy of neutrality . . . is the only one possible," to one where the United Nations is an active proponent of studies of action programs in the field of population, and may soon reach agreement on participation in such programs.

This leads inevitably to Latin-American attitudes. In Latin America both culture and religion long led to a belief that any proposal for restrictions on fertility would be repudiated. But the Latin Americans also are realizing that they face a problem. In the field of morality they are shocked to learn from recent studies that large numbers of women are resorting to illegal abortions to avoid more children. It is worth noting that at the first of what is proposed to be at least ten annual meetings of the Catholic Inter-American Cooperation Programme, which was held in Chicago in February 1964, the statement was made that population growth is an important factor in the whole problem of Latin America, and there was no dissent. Moreover, the Latin-American nations who had been a part of a solid bloc opposed to United Nations action have, over the last four years, either voted for action by the United Nations on population or abstained in increasing numbers. At a meeting at the Pan-American Union in September of 1964, where the whole question of population was discussed before a large number of the ambassadors to the Organization of American States, no one questioned that this was an important problem demanding attention. This new Latin-American attitude and interest are reflected in the October 5, 1964, *Weekly Newsletter* of the Alliance for Progress, which opens with the following: "The Alliance's emphasis on long-range economic and social planning is focus-ing attention as never before on the problem of Latin America's expanding population." It then devotes half of its four-page issue to the problem presented by expanded popula-tion, not in terms of food supply alone but in terms of the effects of such growth on all efforts to promote social and economic progress in Latin America.

Public Discussion

The Population Dilemma, a publication of the American Assembly of Columbia University under the chairmanship of Henry M. Wriston, was published in 1963. This book was the basis for the first American Assembly on population—the twenty-third American Assembly—held at Arden House at Harriman, New York, from May 2–5, 1963. This meeting has already been followed by seven regional assemblies held in San Francisco under the sponsorship of the World Affairs Council of Northern California from June 27–29, 1963; in the Wash-ington area under the sponsorship of the George Washington University from November 14–17, 1963; at Palm Springs, California, from November 28 to December 1, 1963, under the sponsorship of Occidental College; in New Orleans under the sponsorship of Tulane University, from January 30 to February 2, 1964; in the northwest at the University of Oregon, from February 6–9, 1964; in the Midwest at the University of Missouri from February 13–16, 1964; in New England, under the sponsorship of the World Affairs Council of Boston, from April 16–18, 1964; and finally, by the Asso-ciated Colleges of the Midwest under the sponsorship of the Johnson Foundation, Racine, Wisconsin, at Wingspread, April 16–19, 1964. The attitudes expressed by the participants in the National Assembly and in the regional assemblies varied greatly, but, with the exception of a minority report in the last cited, there was general agreement that rapid population growth in the world posed the United States a very serious problem demanding attention. Happily, most of these groups recognized the delicacy of the problem and the need, in facing it, to pay attention to the rights of individuals.

In the annual conference of the Committee for International Economic Growth in 1963, there was, for the first time in its activities, a special panel devoted to this question of population and economic growth. Here we have a group devoted to the question of improving the lot of man in the underdeveloped countries, speaking for the first time on the question of population. The Society for International Development in the same year had, again for the first time, a panel devoted to the question of population. In their conferences, therefore, two of the major national organizations dealing with the question of international economic growth and foreign aid have admitted the relevance of including a discussion of the question of population.

Mass-Media Treatment

The growth of interest in the question of population in our society has been reflected in the mass media. More and more newspapers include articles concerning the population question. One can hardly visit the magazine stand on any given week without finding at least one magazine, often a mass-circulation periodical, with an article on the same problem. There is a tendency for many of the popular magazines to treat this in a rather limited and cavalier fashion, as a conflict between the Catholic position and others. This treatment may take the form of a pathetic plea by a Catholic mother, as in the *Saturday Evening Post* for April 4, 1964, or a suggestion by implication, as in an article entitled "The Church and the Pill" in *The Nation* for October 5, 1964, that the population question is now one which must be solved by the Catholic Church through a change in its position on the use of contraceptives. *Cosmopolitan*, in its issue of September 1964, carries a long article on "Catholics and Birth Control"—a rather balanced presentation, but one that nevertheless suggests that the only thing standing in the way of an effective approach to the population question is the position taken by the Catholic Church.

Other periodicals, such as *McLean's*, a Canadian magazine, present more concise information on the importance of the population problem, as in an article entitled "The Birth Control Explosion" in the issue of March 21, 1964. In this article the question is raised as to whether foreign aid can hope to raise living standards in underdeveloped countries unless birth control is practiced, so that increases in growth are not eaten up by an even larger expansion of population. *Science*, in its May 1, 1964 issue, speaks hopefully of the success of the activities of the International Planned Parenthood Federation in Latin America following its meeting in Puerto Rico and the indication that the American aid agency, the Agency for International Development, was prepared to move in on birth control in that area.

Going back a little further, the *Saturday Review* of February 16, 1963, has an article by Grenville Clark entitled "Solving the Inhuman Equation." This is a thoughtful treatment of the relation of the problem of nuclear war and the population explosion. "The two paramount problems of our time, which in some way affect all the people of the world," says the author, "are the problem of preventing nuclear war and the problem of population control." Marya Mannes, in an article in the August 15, 1964, issue of *Vogue* in turn insists that after the bomb, rapid growth of population is the most important problem facing our society.

Getting a little further from the mass media, but still of popular significance, the 1964 *World Year Book* publishes an article entitled "Population Boom . . . or Boomerang," subtitled "The World Faces a Man-Made Crisis—'Population Explosion.'" This asks whether or not man can "use the same science and technology that created the problem to solve it? Or will hunger and poverty sweep across the face of the world?" *Life, Look,* and *The Reader's Digest* all have had articles in recent months on the subject.

Catholic magazines have also become interested and involved in this question. The *Commonweal* devoted the entire issue of June 5, 1964, to the question of "Responsible Parenthood." This discussion covers a wide range of opinion, reflects the complexity of the problem for the individual and the world, and suggests questions to be considered, without presuming to offer any simple, easy answers. The same magazine, in its October 9, 1964, issue, considers editorially another aspect of the population problem under the heading "Race Against Hunger," concluding that some form of family limitation is essential and must be actively encouraged. "The theologians" the editorial continues, "can and should argue about what means of achieving this are moral, but it would be foolish for any of us to close our eyes to the gravity of the problem we face." In the December 1963 issue of *Jubilee* two articles—one by a Catholic mother, one by a Catholic father—asked for a clarification and restatement of the Church's teaching on marriage, sex, and birth control in the light of current developments, not only in theology, but also in science, medicine, and psychology. *Jubilee* invited its readers to comment on the article, and in its June 1964 issue devoted some seventeen pages to comments received from its readers.

That Latin-American countries have begun to think seriously about this problem is also reflected in the mass media. The magazine *Vision* has instituted in *Progress* what it hopes to be the yearbook on Latin America. The lead article in the new yearbook, by Alberto Lleras Camargo, former president of Colombia, starts out with a statement that "there is a crisis today, brought on by the population explosion that is going on mainly in the racially mixed, tropical, extremely poor belt that circles the globe and separates the two white zones of the earth—the industrial, the rich region of the North and that of the far South." He goes on to say that "the peoples of the hemisphere will not be able to accomplish the great things they set out to do under the Alliance unless there is a full and frank airing of one of the main causes of social sickness and economic waste—the huge increase in the number of people. This problem had been noted hundreds of times in passing or as a side issue; it has not been analyzed fully or in its own right. This is the cause of much of the unrest, frustration, and the near despair which are wreaking more havoc among the leadership elements than among the masses, who are not equipped to understand the real source of their plight and simply attribute it to the government in power."

There have, of course, been dissents to proposals to restrict population growth, but even these recognize there is a problem. In *Report* for June 1964, which devotes itself to the topic "Population—The Real Issues," the lead article is entitled "When Demography Becomes Demagoguery." Barbara Ward is quoted on the responsibility of the rich countries doing

something to help the poor countries and, finally, it is suggested that the idea of restricting population growth is "a
negative solution arising from a shortsighted, stopgap men-
tality." The article goes on to say that "in a final analysis, the
birth-control proposal covers up a defeatist attitude, which
fails to take into account the resources and potentialities
latent in the whole of nature including man himself." It
suggests that growth of population is a great challenge to our
people, to all of the peoples of the world, to make the social
and personal changes required so that our technology can be
applied to our resources in such a way that all men may be
adequately taken care of, rather than in an attempt to restrict
increases in population.

The London *Economist* for September 5, 1964, in an article
entitled "People, Not Population," takes a quiet, concise, hard
look at the problem posed by rapidly rising population. It
recognizes the dangers posed by rapid population growth,
both in the underdeveloped and the developed countries, and
concludes: "Man will need to control his nature and his habits
of procreation if they are not to control him but, life being as
infinitely complicated as it is, one can only feel one's way
piecemeal toward the kinds of control that will do more good
than harm. At least we should start genuinely examining the
problems now instead of putting our heads in the sands of an
inherited and now uneasy optimism. In the early nineteenth
century the slums themselves were regarded as an aspect of
progress."

This is by no means an exhaustive review. It is meant only
to illustrate the attention recently given by mass media and
certain other influential journals to the population question.
Since magazines and newspapers do not ordinarily use space
on subjects unless sizable segments of the population are

interested in them, this recent expanded treatment of the population question would seem to indicate an increase of interest in it by our society.

Action Programs

Fertility Control. There has been a considerable expansion in activities related to the control of fertility over recent years. The International Planned Parenthood Association has steadily expanded its activities abroad, most recently in Latin America, with increasing attention and success. The Ford Foundation also expanded its activities, setting up in 1963 a separate organizational unit responsible for population programs. In its annual report for 1963 the Rockefeller Foundation, reassessing its activities over the years, established new orders of priorities for its activities. Concerning the population problem, it came to the conclusion that "an increasing number of thoughtful persons agree that no greater challenge faces mankind than the stabilization of population. The rate at which new individuals are coming into the world each day is stark evidence that sheer numbers may so overburden resources that social progress will grind to a halt." The report announced that its board of trustees had, in a policy document entitled "Plans for the Future," decided to include the population problem under the five areas of concentration to which it would devote priority attention. It should be noted that another of the five areas was "Toward the Conquest of Hunger." As to the action proposed, the Foundation announced that the factors involved are many and complex and must be approached from various points of view and that it would, therefore, assist (1) research relating to human fertility; (2) research in demography and on cultural attitudes;

and (3) pilot operations and studies in areas where population density poses an especially difficult problem and where there is a desire for help.

The report of the Population Council for 1962–1963 states that "during the two years under review, 1962–1963, a turning point was passed in general public awareness of the problems of population growth. These years, which close the first decade of the Council's work, brought widespread public understanding that rising rates of population growth are serious threats to human welfare in much of the world. The views of scientists became the views of the people, at least enough people to influence national decisions in enough nations to make an impact on the world." The Council carries out research programs in demography and training programs for advanced graduate studies in population for personnel from Asia, Africa, and Latin America. In the two years under review the Council strengthened its support of these programs. It makes research grants for demographic research, and provides technical assistance and research in family planning. It was active in the period under review in Pakistan, Korea, Taiwan, Tunisia, Turkey, and the United States with studies of potential or actual family planning programs. It supports studies in fertility control, aimed at gaining greater knowledge of human physiology and fertility and the development of devices or methods to control fertility. Its annual budget has grown from $147,000 in 1953 to $5,591,000 of expenditures in 1963. Funds were provided by The Ford Foundation, but also by numerous other contributors. Approximately one-half of the funds for 1963 were contributed by The Ford Foundation. The remainder was furnished by a number of other foundations and private individuals.

Thus, over recent years, action programs and research programs have been stepped up in response to growing public recognition and growing acceptance in a number of countries of the idea that birth rates must be controlled. In December 1962 the General Assembly of the United Nations voted down a resolution that that organization should give technical assistance for national projects and programs dealing with the problem of population. In the same month, however, an official representative of the United States, speaking before the United Nations Economic Committee, expressed the concern of the United States with America's population trends, as well as those of the less developed countries, and while stating that "the population policy of any country must be determined by that country and that country alone," went on to say that "the United States believes that obstacles should not be placed in the way of other governments which, in the light of their own economic needs and culture and religious values, seek solution to their population problem." He added that "the United States hoped that the valuable efforts of the United Nations in the population field might be substantially expanded."

This was followed by an announcement by the Agency for International Development that requests from developing countries concerning the social and biological aspects of the population problem would be referred to the United States Public Health Service and the Children's Bureau. It was also announced that the United States was making a contribution of $500,000 to the World Health Organization for research on human reproduction, and the Agency for International Development appointed a demographic consultant. While national governmental organizations, with the exception of a few like Sweden, have not yet very actively entered the field, it seems certain that the United States will soon go on to more extensive assistance to countries seeking to control fertility. It is altogether probable that the United Nations will also, very soon, have an active program of this same nature, quite apart from the important demographic work it has long carried on.

A number of states have established programs to control population growth. That of Puerto Rico has long been widely reported. In December 1963 the first Asian Population Conference was held in New Delhi under the joint sponsorship of the United Nations Economic Committee for Asia and the Far East and the United Nations Bureau of Technical Assistance Operations, with the cooperation of the government of India. The keynote speeches indicated that the purpose of the conference was to explore means of checking population growth in order to make economic development of greater benefit to the people of the area; this approach was not acceptable to a number of the participating countries, however. As the conference continued, the complexity of the problem of population growth was recognized, and it was seen that the problem differed for each country. This conference, where efforts at population control by a number of countries was discussed, was apparently a sobering experience; it led to conclusions that family planning alone is not the answer but, at the least, must be accompanied by great social changes leading to a better use of resources. A useful brief report is contained in the February–March issue of *Social Action*, a publication of the Indian Social Institute. This contains summaries for each participating country, most of which indicate whether, and sometimes to what extent, the governments have programs to limit population growth.

Freedom from Hunger Campaign. One of the questions most often raised when rapid population growth is discussed is whether or not food production is keeping pace with and can be expected to keep pace with such growth. The problem of improving world nutritional standards has been a preoccupation of international agencies since the days of the League of Nations. The United Nations, many of its specialized agencies, and a number of national foreign-aid programs have been providing assistance to developing countries in the agricultural field for many years.

In 1960 a five-year Freedom from Hunger Campaign was initiated by the Food and Agriculture Organization (FAO) with the cooperation of other specialized agencies of the United Nations. The FAO has made three studies of hunger in the world since the last war. These World Food surveys were made in 1946, 1952, and 1963. The last study reveals that from one-third to one-half of the world's population, that is, between one billion and one and a half billion people, still suffer from hunger and malnutrition. It also suggests that world food supplies would have to be more than doubled by 1980 and tripled by the turn of the century in order to bring about a moderate improvement in the level of nutrition of the peoples of the world. The report recognizes that the problem is different in different regions, that greater problems exist in some than in others, and that greater efforts may be required in some than in others. In its section on "The Possibilities of Producing the Required Food," the following conclusion is reached:

Production possibilities were kept in mind when setting up the short-term targets, but one is left wondering whether the large increases can in fact be achieved over a decade or so. These doubts may be even stronger in the case of the more distant objective. But there should be little room for doubt on one score: the world could grow enough food to meet all these needs if we made rational use of nature's bounty. Doubts arise because the necessary effort to reach the targets may not be made. Other objectives may cloud the horizon: the financial resources required to develop the world's agriculture may not be made available; the incentive to expand production may be absent in many parts of the developing world, and the underdeveloped countries may be unable to purchase the food supplies they require.

Major activities in technical and financial assistance over many years and the distribution of surplus food supplies from developed countries have not yet made it possible to assure adequate food to our increasing world population. Despite belief in our technical capacity to meet these needs, serious doubt remains that they will in fact be used.

Population, Peace, and Christian Responsibilities: A Morally Acceptable Public Policy

Robert F. Drinan, S.J.

It appears certain that within the near future Catholics will both be requested by non-Catholics and required by their own moral principles to enunciate a position on what would be an acceptable public policy for America with regard to state-sponsored distribution of birth-control information and devices. The question is likely to arise in so many different ways that it seems impossible to formulate one general Catholic viewpoint which would be applicable to all or most situations. Perhaps it might be helpful, therefore, if we sketch out the several ways in which basic issues about public policy regarding planned parenthood might arise. While outlining these possibilities, we will discuss the positions which Catholics might assume with respect to each situation.

Basic issues relating to proposed legal regulation of birth control could arise in the following ways:

1. State and Federal Legislation

Although contraceptives are reported to be as readily available for purchase as most other standard medical items, it is seldom noted that their sale and merchandising are, unlike any other comparable item, surrounded by secrecy and an almost complete blackout on advertising of any kind. The motivations for this semi-clandestine approach derive apparently from a collective modesty or shame as well as from a fear of violating the federal Comstock Act and similar state laws regulating the sale of contraceptives.

One of the many anomalies in the curious history of the law's regulation of the distribution of contraceptives is the vigorous assault on state laws restricting the sale of birth-control devices but the relatively unchallenged continuation of a federal law enacted during the last half of the nineteenth century. While the federal law is almost totally unenforced—and is probably unenforceable—its existence is at least a symbol of a national policy which Congress presumably is unwilling to repeal.

Another anomaly in the area of state legislation is the strange reasoning by which legislatures and courts permit the sale of contraceptives—even in some states by means of a vending machine—for the purpose of preventing the spread of a communicable disease. It was this curious argument that was accepted by the Supreme Court of Massachusetts in a case in which the defendant-vendor of contraceptives was acquitted and the Massachusetts law on the matter was virtually nullified.

Catholics have not officially endorsed any existing state law forbidding or restricting the sale of contraceptives since the last controversy on this matter in Massachusetts in 1948. The court cases challenging the Connecticut law which restricts the use or sale of contraceptives have not caused Catholic spokesmen to take any official position; it is frequently stated or assumed, however, by many non-Catholics that Catholic officials in Connecticut support the existing law. The announced intervention as *amicus curiae* of the National Catholic Council on Civil Liberties on behalf of the convicted defendants in the current Connecticut case may indicate a development in Catholic thinking of some significance.

What norms should Catholics employ when they take a position on state and federal laws regulating the distribution of contraceptives? One position could be the not unreasonable stance that, although these laws are archaic and perhaps anachronistic in their purposes and wording, they represent a public morality attained in a pan-Protestant nation which coincides with contemporary Catholic moral thought; Catholics consequently, according to this approach to the problem, should oppose the repeal of these laws or at least should not acquiesce in their repeal without some protest.

A second position would be an attempt to resist the wholesale repeal of a law by advocating a modern and modified statute which would limit the sale of contraceptives to persons with a doctor's prescription, or who at least gave evidence that they were married. One could argue, to be sure, that such a law could not be enforced even if enacted and that, furthermore, Catholics, by urging such a statute, would be open to the charge that they are seeking to impose their own moral norms on non-Catholics.

A third position would affirmatively urge the repeal of present laws restricting the sale of contraceptives. This posture would be justified by the reasoning that such a law which is so at variance with the overwhelming consensus of most non-Catholics in America has no chance of establishing a public policy which could be an enforceable norm of general behavior.

Any one of these three positions—or variations of them—is open to Catholics. The question of the need and wisdom of civil legislation restricting the distribution of contraceptives has no one answer in Catholic theology or philosophy; it is a question whose resolution must be governed by jurisprudential norms regarding the purposes of law and the extent to which a law, based on a moral concept but without a substantial consensus of agreement by the majority of its intended subjects, can be wisely enacted and enforced.

Catholics, therefore, should not insist that *one* of the above approaches is *the* Catholic position. Nor should non-Catholics rebuke advocates of any of these three positions. Endorsement of any one of these three views does not compromise Catholic principles or neglect what Catholics should do to strengthen public morality.

2. *Tax Money for Programs of Planned Parenthood*

A more difficult moral problem confronts Catholics with regard to the rapidly emerging question of the use of tax support for the purpose of promoting programs of planned parenthood. This question can arise in several contexts necessitating different responses from Catholics.

In the controversies to date about the adoption of legislation or of an administrative policy permitting government-sponsored agencies to distribute birth-control information and devices Catholics have argued against such a policy on the basis of three principal contentions:

1) It is unjust to take the tax money contributed by Catholics and spend it in part to promote a practice which for Catholics is inherently immoral.

2) By the financing of birth-control clinics the state in effect endorses and adopts one particular view of a disputed moral question; such a course of action is unfair to those whose moral viewpoint is rejected.

3) When a state subsidizes birth control its prestige and influence are so committed to a particular point of view that to a certain degree the state *teaches* this view as morally

correct. As a result some individuals whose religious creed forbids the use of contraceptives may be induced to use these devices because of the strong but less than coercive pressure of a state-sponsored social-welfare agency.

Controversies over the use of public funds for birth-control purposes are of such recent origin that there has not been time for a highly developed Catholic position to emerge. Once again the clashing moral principles and the sociological imponderables can lead Catholics to varying positions. Let us therefore analyze each of the three contentions set out above; our purpose will be to determine whether or not one or all of the objections raised by Catholics poses a problem of a minority group which should deter the state from pursuing a goal contrary to the beliefs of this minority.

1) Can Catholics legitimately and reasonably seek to prevent the use of tax money for birth-control purposes? If they can do so and still be advocates of an ordered and pluralistic society then it would appear that public support of contraception is, according to Catholic morality, far more objectionable than tax exemption and other privileges for non-Catholic churches and schools. There is, of course, a difference in these two matters in that the Catholic Church also benefits from the tax-exemption privileges extended to all religious groups.

Pursuing this analogy a bit further, we can wonder whether Catholics would extend their endorsement of tax exemption for *all* religious groups to birth-control clinics if information about "rhythm" were given equal facilities and proportionate funds. In other words, if Catholics approve and indeed endorse tax exemption for churches which teach "heresy," is it consistent for Catholics to insist that the state may not assist a form of family planning unacceptable to Catholics if the state gives proportionate benefits to a program of fertility control acceptable to the Catholic conscience?

The basic question, therefore, is the extent and the nature of the protest which one group of taxpayers may responsibly make concerning the expenditure of tax money for purposes deemed by this particular minority group to be immoral. One thinks of the position of the Christian Scientists protesting the fluoridation of water, the Quakers objecting to military service, or the Amish refusing to participate in social security. These examples, however, are importantly different from state action designed to control population because, when the modern state assumes the obligation of implementing a policy of regulating population, it can rely upon the endorsement of this ultimate objective by many groups—religious and secular, Catholic and non-Catholic. The exploding population of the world, in other words, has prompted many if not most responsible persons to come to the conclusion that the nations of the earth have at least *some* obligation to control human fertility and to regulate the world's expanding population.

The moral issue is not the undisputed right and duty of an ordered society to prevent its destruction by excessive reproduction. The moral issue is rather the legitimacy of the means which may be adopted to achieve this objective. Catholics are not and cannot be opposed to a nation's efforts to prevent its self-strangulation by excessive reproduction; Catholics are opposed only to the concept of the state using its enormous influence and prestige to endorse immoral methods of family limitation.

If Catholics begin with the principle that the modern state has *some* duty to try to resolve the problem of a runaway world population, Catholics might not end at the narrow and negative position that the expenditure of tax monies for birth-control clinics is a policy which is unjust to Catholics.

It appears, therefore, that the simple contention that the expenditure of tax money for the advancement of contraception is unfair to Catholics cannot survive a critical analysis. Such a contention would, however, have merit if the state refused to recognize or to provide for the conscience of those for whom artificial birth control is morally unacceptable.

2) The second objection to state support for family planning urged by some Catholics again confuses ends and means. This second argument asserts that state neutrality toward a moral issue is violated even by the state's advocacy of population regulation in general. Catholics presumably would not object to tax support for family planning if the state restricted its activities solely to an explanation of the rhythm method. But clearly non-Catholics would protest such an arrangement on the basis that the state, by endorsing *only* rhythm in order to maintain neutrality, would in effect be rejecting neutrality by preferring natural over artificial birth control.

The basic issue, therefore, comes to this: does the modern state have a right to take the position that it will assist *all* persons to plan their families, but only in ways consistent with their religious beliefs?

If one denies the existence of such a right in the modern state, one must then reply to the question whether the denial of such a right in effect imputes to the state the non-neutral attitude that overpopulation is not a problem of such moral importance as to justify state intervention in its resolution. The exploding population of the world, in other words, and the tragedy of more than one billion human beings living on a substandard diet can hardly be said to be a problem on which the modern state can be neutral by being inactive. To be inactive is to reject the counsels of the vast majority of demographers, humanitarians, and indeed of churchmen who feel that a national and international program of fertility control is required by the elementary canons of common sense and human dignity.

It appears that when some Catholics object to every form of participation by the state in the distribution of information regarding family planning they are saying in effect that the entire area of the regulation of population is either too sacred for state intervention or too free of difficulties to require state assistance.

The question which contemporary Catholic thought has not yet explored is the teaching of the natural moral law regarding the duty of individuals, nations, and international society in general to regulate and to limit the reproductive rate in order to avoid a globe so fully populated that a truly human and virtuous life will not be possible for the vast majority of men. No one claims that any specific formulation of a moral principle on this vast subject can be ascertained from the natural law by some rapid process of analysis. But if Catholics *started* from this point rather than from the point of a moral ban on contraceptives Catholic thought regarding a public policy designed to regulate fertility might be much more positive, constructive, and indeed more in conformity with a broader and deeper understanding of the more profound dimensions of the natural moral law.

It is a misleading oversimplification to assert, as many Catholics do, that the natural law forbids the use of artificial birth control and that therefore the state may not ethically encourage or promote family limitation. The fact is that the natural law also teaches that society has some obligation to regulate an increase in population in order to prevent the development of malnutrition and the other undesirable consequences of a rising and uncontrolled population. Even though the natural law's prohibition of artificial birth control appears to be clearer and more definite than the natural law's imposition of an affirmative obligation to regulate population, it is nonetheless a distortion of the objective moral order to hold that the only duty with respect to population limitation placed on public officials by the natural law is the obligation not to encourage the use of contraceptives.

The state consequently has the same duty which every parent has—the obligation not to bring into the world more children than a particular parent can reasonably bring up and properly educate. No one claims that any specific recommendation involving actual numbers is knowable merely from the natural law—either for parents or much less for the state. But the principle itself seems to be indisputably a logical inference from the natural moral law.

If it is conceded, therefore, that the state shares in the duties imposed on parents by nature itself of responsibly limiting the size of their families, can Catholics insist that the state carry out its obligation by endorsing only the techniques of natural or rhythm birth control? To state the question seems almost to answer it. For Catholics to take such a position would be the equivalent of asserting that the immorality of artificial birth control is so clearly knowable from reason unaided by Revelation that even the modern secular state, constitutionally neutralized as between religion and irreligion, must logically consider contraception to be as immoral as murder, abortion, or theft. Surely such a position cannot be defended if one considers the totality of all the inferences from the natural law with respect to society's obligations as it confronts the most rapid and the spectacular growth in population in the history of the world.

3) The third objection urged by Catholics in opposing state-sponsored family planning programs centers on the pressure and even quasi-coercion on parents which would assertedly arise as a result of an official state policy endorsing planned parenthood. Upon analysis this objection can perhaps be reduced to the age-old fear that the morality of the majority

if it is not repudiated by the state is likely to influence and even to corrupt the morality of a minority. No one can deny the validity of the fear—especially where, as in the matter under discussion, the American state, for the first time in history, subscribes to the principle that the state should assist parents in carrying out their obligation to bring into the world only that number of children who can be reasonably educated by them and appropriately accommodated by society.

But would not state sponsorship of responsible family planning and fertility control be simply one more pressure added to the already countless direct and indirect forces that implicitly teach that the spacing and limitation of one's family are desirable objectives? In a negative way the American government has already sided with these forces in its failure to have a plan of family allowances—a program in effect in more than forty of the leading and most progressive nations of the earth. In a more positive way the American government, both federal and state, has conceded the importance of family planning by refusing to enforce the Comstock Act and comparable state anti-contraceptive legislation.

The acceptance or at least the toleration by the American state of the concept of the desirability of fertility regulation is attributable to the ever clearer need for *some* type of population control as well as to the overwhelming consensus on this matter of almost all non-Catholic Americans.

Is it realistic, therefore, and indeed is it fair for some Catholics to take the position that the mere intervention of the state as another agency encouraging family planning— whether by mechanical or natural means—exerts coercion on Catholics to indulge in practices contrary to their creed and their conscience? It is, of course, granted that the Church and all Catholics have a prophetic role to fulfill and a duty to preach to an erring society the truths of reason and revelation.

The newly realized truth, however, which must be reconciled with the Church's traditional role of prophetic teaching regarding the immorality of artificial birth control is the undeniable necessity of regulating the world's exploding population.

The possibility of pressure and even coercion in any state-operated birth-control clinic is, however, a reasonable and well-founded fear on the part of Catholics. Such pressure is most likely to affect the very Catholics who in all probability might be expected to be the principal clients of state birth-control agencies—the poor and the uneducated. But because of this almost inevitable eventuality it does not seem logical, fair, or wise for Catholics to oppose completely all efforts by the state to bring about a more orderly family life where this desirable objective is possible.

3. America's Policy on Foreign Aid and Fertility Control

An intelligent, courageous, but prudent position with regard to existing birth-control legislation can be attained by Catholics without any insurmountable obstacle either in logic or in conscience. Similarly an uncompromising but realistic position can be reached regarding the sponsorship by the state of programs designed to demonstrate in appropriate cases both artificial and natural methods of birth prevention.

The third and most difficult problem, however, involves the attitude which Catholics should adopt in the event that the United States Government introduces into its foreign-aid program a plan to bring birth-control information to those countries which are the recipients of non-military technical assistance.

The familiar bromide recommended to avoid even thinking about this question is the bland suggestion that the United

States Government hand over a certain amount of money to foreign countries so that these nations and not the United States make the decision as to the need for a program of birth prevention. It would indeed be fortunate if America could settle this question by simply allowing other nations to settle it for themselves. While there is unanimity that we should never condone or permit the American government to impose a program of fertility control upon an unwilling nation, there is a striking lack of unanimity as to what America should do if a foreign nation requests a program of fertility control or at least has such an obvious need for such a program that it would accept and even welcome American initiative designed to structure such a program.

American Catholics cannot resolve this third or international phase of the fertility control according to the same assumptions from which an accommodation to state-sponsored birth-control programs in America can be derived. The crucial difference is the fact that the American government, in assisting plans of population limitation within the fifty states, does not necessarily teach as morally correct or incorrect either mechanical or natural birth control; the state in America merely concurs in the desire of most of its citizens to plan their families responsibly and then allows the individual citizen to choose the method that is consistent with his conscience.

In most foreign nations which receive technical assistance from the United States a very different situation is present. In these nations a widespread desire to plan families and to regulate population is not always present and is seldom highly developed. Because of this fact the peoples of these nations have not arrived at any conclusions regarding the morality of artificial or natural methods of birth control. The United States agency which initiates a program of planned parenthood in a nation receiving non-military technical assistance would, almost inevitably, be establishing within that nation a hitherto-unknown moral concept. That concept would teach at least the following principles:

1) It is immoral for individuals or nations to permit the birth of human beings for whom a reasonable education and a decent livelihood will not be available.

2) Parents have the right and the duty to limit the number of their children either by mechanical or by natural methods of birth control.

Government-sponsored American agencies abroad would consequently be teaching the legitimacy of population regulation as well as the morality either of artificial or natural means of birth limitation. It is one thing for a state to accept a moral attitude arrived at by the majority of its people and quite another thing for a state to create or to transfer a set of moral principles to a people who have not previously concurred in these moral principles and who, in fact, have not really been given the option of so concurring.

The critical question which will soon confront Catholics, then, is the position which American Catholics should adopt if America's program of foreign aid should more and more include plans of fertility control to be carried out with American money and personnel. Persuasive arguments can be advanced for the proposition that the impact of the economic aid given to underdeveloped nations by the United States could be almost destroyed by an exploding population within the assisted nation. This same line of reasoning could lead to the conclusion that the United States cannot responsibly give massive economic aid to a nation without ascertaining beforehand the predictable population of the country within the next twenty or thirty years.

All of these factors, however, do not resolve the dilemmas

surrounding the morality of America's introducing into non-European countries the practice of birth regulation. It must be remembered that the widespread approval of contraception now prevalent in Europe and America is not a moral tenet which has been accepted from time immemorial; it is rather the product of only the last generation and is a conclusion accepted by many with reluctance and even with a certain tentativeness. Teaching this attitude toward family planning, therefore, to newly emerged nations of Asia and Africa is a venture that is not free of moral ambiguities.

In view of the newness of the problem of including fertility control in America's foreign-aid program and, furthermore, in view of the nonexistence of an actual problem at this time to be resolved, perhaps the most that one can say about any future Catholic reaction is to express the hope that, when this attitude is formed, it will reflect not merely the natural law's dictates about birth control but also the same law's directives about irresponsible parenthood and the state's duty to regulate it.

Finally, let us hope that Catholics will boldly confront the problem of the world's exploding population and at least concede the possibility that a program of fertility control will still be necessary even after that day of miracles arrives when there is effective national and international economic planning and an adequate distribution of food and land for everyone.

Conclusions

It will be clear from the foregoing and from the paucity of literature by Catholics on world-population problems that Catholics in general have not appreciated the urgency of the pressures and dilemmas surrounding this problem. In the near future Catholics will more and more be virtually forced to concern themselves with the consequences of a rocketing population. Several moral principles must be fully considered and harmonized before any prudential judgment can be reached. But at least the following counsels seem relevant and noteworthy at this point of the development of Catholic thought on this issue.

1) One's attitude toward family planning depends profoundly on one's concept of the family. It is questionable whether the Catholic case against contraception has been clearly expressed in the context of the highly developed Catholic theology of the family. Indeed it often appears that the proponents of birth control emerge in public opinion as the defenders of the stability and solidarity of family life while the opponents of contraception are characterized as persons who would permit the onrush of those very forces which disrupt family life.

In taking positions on the law and birth control, Catholics must search for a new rationale, a deeper view of birth regulation as sometimes necessary to family solidarity, and a more positive conviction that an unregulated birth rate can lead to an erosion of family stability.

2) In making judgments and recommendations regarding a legal policy on family planning, all of us must recognize that we know very little about the effect of the presence or absence of law in this area. In the nature of things no law can do very much to regulate acts which are totally private, nor can any law have much effect if it is substantially at variance with the minds of those whose conduct it is intended to guide.

Catholics, furthermore, have very little experience or background in molding American legal institutions. Catholics have never affirmatively sought the repeal of the many laws permitting conduct contrary to the natural law, such as divorce and sterilization. Catholics have taken a position on America's legal institutions only when a particular group of non-Catholics has sought to weaken the legal-moral consensus written into law when America was a pan-Protestant country.

Catholics consequently should draw conclusions and make recommendations about existing or proposed American laws regulating family life only with an appropriate tentativeness and open-mindedness.

3) All of us finally must regularly recall that the dimensions and implications of cultural and religious pluralism on a national and international scale are as yet very dimly perceived. Catholics, as the inheritors of a rich tradition of truths and moral principles derived from both reason and revelation, may have more difficulty than non-Catholics in appreciating the commitment which Vatican Council II will hopefully make—the commitment of Catholics to a profound respect for the fullest religious and cultural freedom for all men.

In thinking of the problems associated with an exploding world population, it might be very helpful if Catholics would begin by considering both the principle that responsible parenthood is indeed a moral imperative and the commitment which the Church has made to respect and honor the religious liberty of all men. If Catholic thought on fertility control commenced with these two moral principles it might result in judgments substantially different from many of the conclusions enunciated by Catholics up to this point in the ongoing world-wide debate regarding what humanity should do to prevent its own suicide by overpopulation.

A Spirit of Enlarged Freedom

Terrence J. Murphy

The Church at this hour is engaged in a great historic renewal of her interior life and a reassessment of her role "in the world but not of the world." Vatican Council II is not a change in direction so much as a change in emphasis resulting from new reflection by the Church on her inmost being and life. The end result of this deepening of her own consciousness and rededication cannot now be fully foreseen. The Church will have to run her historic course for some years before it will be possible to assess adequately the extent of this "updating." But the evidence indicates that the "People of God" are achieving new insight into their dignity, their potentialities, and their destiny which will be embodied in new structures and in a new spirit which are likely to perdure for many decades, perhaps for centuries. At the moment there is every reason to believe that the dream of Pope John for an "updating" will be more than realized. Not only has the Church come abreast of the modern world but she bids well to assume a new position of real influence.

Vatican Council II is many things, but surely one of its chief characteristics is a spirit of enlarged freedom. The first two sessions of the Council were periods of testing and probing, of searching for a consensus beneath the sometimes strident and sometimes conflicting voices. That consensus has become clearly manifest in the third session. The Council Fathers know where they wish to lead God's people. They have agreed upon the general plan of the "*aggiornamento*," clearly see the interrelationship of all segments of this program, and know the spirit with which it must be suffused. That spirit is one of openness. Evidence of this freedom and openness is found in every schema of the Council.

The constitution on the liturgy opens wide the door not only to changes in the language and the form of public worship but also to new modes of participation which will likely involve new participants in the conducting of liturgical services. This openness to change will mean a fuller measure of sharing, a fuller freedom, for the laity in the community of worshipers.

The schema on revelation leaves open the question on the relation between Sacred Scripture and tradition. Thereby it enhances the freedom of Catholic scriptural scholars in their dialogue with their Protestant colleagues. The schema on ecumenism considered by the Council Fathers provides for a new measure of freedom, not merely in dialogue but also in religious observances with our separated brethren.

Collegiality combined with national episcopal conferences will introduce greater pluralism in the Church. There will be a freedom for local or national determination of many questions of ecclesiastical polity which now are either not considered open to change or which require permission from the highest central authority.

The Council's discussion of religious liberty is the most explicit treatment of freedom undertaken by the Council. Certainly there exists among the Fathers of the Council a moral unanimity in favor of religious liberty. The American hierarchy was the champion of the Declaration on Religious Liberty when it came up for consideration in the Council chambers. While there was almost unanimous support in favor of full religious freedom, there was disagreement on the basis for this freedom. Those Council Fathers who have been nurtured in the Anglo-Saxon tradition of constitutionalism tend to look upon religious freedom as a constitutional immunity from all coercion in matters of religion. They see this as a requirement for the full development of the human personality and dignity. Council Fathers whose intellectual formation is moored in the tradition of the European continent want a more theological and philosophical underpinning for religious freedom. However this problem may be resolved, it is evident that there is a universal agreement in favor of religious liberty for all men.

In the Declaration on the Jews the Council Fathers have displayed their concern for the rights and freedom of others and for rooting out the causes of discrimination and prejudice.

The Council Fathers are considering the role of the laity in three separate aspects, their role in the Church, their role in the world, and the apostolate of the laity in itself. From the Council will probably come a statement which describes the laity, not in terms of sharing in the apostolate of the hierarchy, but rather it will speak of the mission of the Church in which all share and then describe the role of the laity, the clergy, and the hierarchy in relation to the Church's apostolate. This shift in viewpoint, which looks at the laity in relation to the mission of the Church rather than in relation to the hierarchy, opens the way for a new measure of freedom and autonomy for the laity.

Moreover, there is a difference between the common priesthood of all who are baptized and by which the baptized are deputed to worship and to teach and the royal priesthood of the laity which is exercised by a life of virtue. That the royal priesthood is distinct from the common priesthood received in

Holy Orders is seen in the fact that it was enjoyed and exercised by the people of the Old Testament, that is, before the institution of the sacraments. The royal priesthood of the laity is concerned with a ministry which is not necessarily connected to the hierarchy. In the order of things temporal it will be seen that the laity, because of their greater knowledge of the temporal order, will more and more make moral judgments and decisions.

The corollary of this spirit of openness and greater freedom, so characteristic of the Second Vatican Council, is an enlargement of our responsibilities. The burden rests more heavily on us to struggle with the problems that confront our society and the Church. While freedom is a fundamental value, it is also a means to an end, that is, to the achievement of a fuller truth and to the enhancement of human dignity. The task before us is to enter into the fresh spirit of freedom, of openness, of inquiry, and dialogue, in order to examine carefully and imaginatively the many aspects of the complex subjects which concern the Catholic Association for International Peace and the thoughtful men of every nation. It is important that we realize the nature of the role we must play in maturing Catholic opinion on such matters as population, nuclear war, and other subjects related to peace.

The temporal order is increasingly seen as the realm proper to the layman. It is here that he enjoys his greatest competency. He has a proper knowledge and understanding of the complexity and of the laws that govern the specialized fields of the temporal order which are not always and perhaps only rarely matched by priest or bishop. True, there are ethical and theological dimensions to his world. But, again, the layman frequently is in a better position to make the practical judgment in applying these principles than is the cleric. However, the magisterium of the Church has the divine commission to teach moral principles. Concern for the development of a better world should not make us overlook this teaching authority nor neglect its counsel.

To stop with this statement would be to oversimplify. We must not think of moral teachings as thoroughly static. They undergo a progressive unfolding as we come to understand better human nature, God's providential design, and the world in which we live. At times moral teachings are in need of reformulation because of changed conditions or better understanding. It is the task of the theologian and the philosopher to study, to discuss, and to develop moral and theological principles and insights. To do this they need the knowledge and professional skills of the experts in the field or discipline in which the moral principles are applicable. When a sufficient intellectual maturing or ripening has taken place on the part of such scholars, their studies must be put at the disposal of those who exercise the magisterium in the Church in order that the leaders may be truly enlightened and properly discharge their teaching function.

The task, then, is a cooperative one. Let us not envisage three totally distinct groups, the layman in the world, the theologian in academia, and the magisterium or official teachers in the Church removed from both. No, each needs the other in order to make a fuller and more fruitful contribution to the Church and the world. Cooperation in earnest searching for God's truth is needed. There is no room for the continued utterance of principles that are not fully relative to the factual situation on the one hand; or, on the other hand, the building up of pressure and tension for a reformulation of principles without contributing to the enlightenment that alone makes possible a new formulation or application.

Knowledge and insight are needed, not vociferous demands and entreaties.

It would be presumptuous at this moment, despite the endless flood of popular articles, to expect from the Vatican Council a definitive statement on population problems. The same can be said of those complex problems that are associated with nuclear weapons and many other questions related to the peace of the world. We have not yet sufficiently done our job of studying and analyzing these problems, in themselves and in the light of our Christian heritage, for the magisterium of the Church to be sufficiently informed and prepared for a new declaration. This underscores the importance of discussion. The task of study, reflection, and of thoughtful discussion has only begun. Let us address ourselves to it with energy and confidence.

Observations and Conclusions

George H. Dunne, S. J.

In the foregoing discussions all those who touched at all upon the long-range problem of the capacity of the world to produce in sufficient quantities to support the populations of the future have agreed with Pope John that there is insufficient data upon which to reach a certain judgment; although there is considerable support for the opinion that the world's potential resources will not be exhausted in the future. On the other hand, all of the contributors to this volume also agree that the immediate problem remains and that it is grave. The rate of growth in underdeveloped areas, canceling out, or virtually canceling out, the socioeconomic development rate which the best efforts can effectuate, seems to condemn a large part of the world to increasing misery and at a period of history when the population of the world is becoming increasingly unwilling to submit to misery.

There would seem to be many people who still labor under the illusion that the population problem can be solved simply by manufacturing contraceptive devices and making them available to the multitudes and teaching the multitudes how to use them. If nothing else, these papers demolish this myth. All of them clearly recognize the complexity of the problem. Dr. Berelson, it is quite obvious, is the most optimistic in this regard in being hopeful of great success in limiting population by the employment of such contraceptive devices, specifically by the inter-uterine device that he mentions. He writes most cheerfully about results already obtained in certain pilot projects and most hopefully about the possibilities of further results in the future. He believes that a large proportion of the people everywhere want family planning now. One notes disagreement here between Dr. Berelson and Father Drinan, who implies that in vast areas of the world that we are dealing with, such as India, this desire does not exist, and it would be an imposition of our own point of view upon these people if we were to attempt to persuade them to resort to contraception. In any event, Dr. Berelson seems to believe that if a large proportion of the people everywhere were able to realize their desires with respect to family planning, "a good deal of the population problem would disappear." Unless I misunderstand them, Dr. Dedrick and Dr. Taeuber reach quite different conclusions.

Dr. Dedrick points out that in Latin America, one of the areas where the population pressure is most critical, there are strong, deeply rooted cultural forces which tend to defeat efforts to limit fertility. Particularly in rural Latin America, according to Dr. Dedrick, the people want many children— the husband because it is a proof of his masculinity and the wife because she is proud to exhibit to her neighbors her virile husband. It may be possible eventually to change such cultural attitudes, but such attitudes are not easily nor soon overcome or changed. And meantime the problem intensifies. Dr. Dedrick calls attention to other cultural factors in Latin America, such as early marriage, the youthfulness of the population entering the labor force, and so on. These factors reveal how wrong they are who think that the answer is simply to make available contraceptives and information on how to use them.

I confess to being one of those who have hoped that the use of oral contraceptives, or "the pill" as it is generally described, would be found a morally acceptable method of bringing population growth under reasonable control. The immorality of contraceptive devices which intervene in the sex act itself consists in this—that they prevent the act from proceeding to its normal end and, the end of a thing being its nature in the Aristotelian phrase, such an intervention is therefore against the nature of the act itself. This, of course, is my own analysis. My view has been that "the pill" does not intervene in the sex act but only fosters the establishing of certain conditions in which, although the act itself is allowed freely to proceed to its normal end, contraception in the absence of ova will not ensue.

This has always been my thinking on the subject, and consequently I have always hoped that eventually the professional moralist would come around to my way of viewing it, and eventually agree with me upon the validity of the distinction which I make, and thus justify morally in given conditions the use of "the pill." I still have that hope. But this alone does not answer the problem. "The pill" has not proved very acceptable in pilot projects; further, even though the fertility rate should be halved in the next thirty-five years, the population of Asia and South Asia, according to Dr. Taeuber, would still double itself in those same years. This alone is enough to open our eyes to the complexity of the problem. It is not simply a matter of reducing the fertility rate. Much more is involved.

There is no single and no simple solution to this extremely complex problem. The contributors to this volume are all aware of how complex the problem really is; this awareness, of course, should lead only to determination on our part to mobilize all of our forces to attack the problem more vigorously. It was not the intention of this conference to produce a solution but merely to broaden our understanding of the dimensions of the problem. Certainly Father Thomas does this when he argues that what is needed is "a thorough reinterpretation of the personal and social significance of human sexuality together with a careful restructuring of the various relationships relevant to its meaningful development, expression, and regulation"—in a word, "the reformulation and cultural implementation of the conception of human sexuality consonant with the destiny of the person and the needs of society under modern conditions."

The problem is indeed complex, and predictions about the future are conjectural, another point made by Dr. Taeuber. Demographers can be wrong, but if there is uncertainty about the long-range future there can be no uncertainty about the immediate problem. A million people *do* sleep in the streets of Calcutta; and people *do* live on a mountain of garbage in the slums outside of Lima, Peru, and slums *do* continue to proliferate in Latin America and in many other parts of the world. The immediate problem exists, however the conjectural and speculative nature of the future may be. A conclusion which one may safely draw from this discussion is that while the search for more reliable and acceptable means of population control must go on, it is essential, as Dr. Taeuber points out, that massive efforts be made to hasten the socioeconomic development of the underdeveloped countries. And here Catholics, as Dr. Shuster urges upon us, can and should "help to improve as rapidly as possible the basic economic and social conditions which breed human despair." While the experts—theologians, doctors, demographers, sociologists, and economists—search for the answers to the problem of population growth, the rest of us can throw our support behind every measure which attacks poverty at home or which, under the auspices of the United Nations or our foreign-aid program, contributes to socioeconomic developments abroad. To educate American Catholics to this responsibility in this respect is itself a formidable undertaking, one which, Dr. Shuster suggests, the Catholic Association for International Peace might undertake as one of its projects.

Mention of foreign aid, of course, raises the question of public policy. Dean Moran gives us an illuminating outline of the history of our transition from a "that's not our business" attitude to the present policy of the United States Government, which is clearly stated by Dr. Gardner. If I understand Dr. Gardner correctly, I, for one, cannot see anything in present United States policy which Catholics could be prevented in conscience from supporting. I understand him to say that the present policy of the United States is to be willing to make available, through the United Nations, information and technical assistance to those countries which ask for them, but *not* to supply any of the contraceptive materials or devices. I cannot see any reason why we, as members of a pluralistic society, cannot support this policy or why we should be obliged to oppose it.

GENERAL BIBLIOGRAPHY

BARCLAY, GEORGE W. *Techniques of Population Analysis.* New York: John Wiley and Sons, 1959.

―――. *Colonial Development and Population in Taiwan.* Princeton: Princeton University Press, 1954.

BELSHAW, HORACE. *Population Growth and Levels of Consumption; with Special Reference to Countries in Asia.* London: George Allen and Unwin, 1956.

BLAKE, JUDITH. *Family Structure in Jamaica: The Social Context of Reproduction.* Glencoe, Illinois: The Free Press, 1961.

BOGUE, DONALD J. *The Population of the United States.* Glencoe, Illinois: The Free Press, 1959.

BROWN, HARRISON. *The Challenge of Man's Future.* New York: The Viking Press, 1954.

BROWN, HARRISON, BONNER, J., and WIER, J. *The Next Hundred Years.* New York: The Viking Press, 1957.

COALE, ANSLEY J., and HOOVER, EDGAR M. *Population Growth and Economic Development in Low-Income Countries.* Princeton: Princeton University Press, 1958.

COOK, ROBERT C. *Human Fertility: The Modern Dilemma.* New York: William Sloane Associates, 1951.

COX, PETER R. *Demography and Addendum to Demography.* (Second edition.) Cambridge: Cambridge University Press, 1957.

DAVIS, KINGSLEY. *The Population of India and Pakistan.* Princeton: Princeton University Press, 1951.

DUBLIN, LOUIS, LOTKA, A. J., and SPIEGELMAN, MORTIMER. *Length of Life.* (Revised edition.) New York: The Ronald Press, 1949.

DURAND, JOHN. *The Labor Force in the United States, 1890–1960.* New York: Social Science Research Council, 1948.

ELDRIDGE, HOPE. *Materials of Demography.* Science Press, 1959.

―――. *Population Policies: A Survey of Recent Developments.* Washington: International Union for the Scientific Study of Population, 1954.

FAGLEY, RICHARD. *Population Explosion and Christian Responsibility.* New York: Oxford University Press, 1960.

FARIS, E. J. *Human Ovulation and Fertility.* Philadelphia: J. B. Lippincott, 1956.

FLUGEL, J. C. *Population and Peace.* London: C. A. Watts, 1947.

FORD, JOHN C., S.J., and KELLY, GERALD, S.J. *Contemporary Moral*

Theology, Vols. I and II. Westminster, Maryland: The Newman Press, 1963.

FRANCIS, ROY G. (ed.). *The Population Ahead*. Minneapolis: University of Minnesota Press, 1958.

FREEDMAN, RONALD, WHELPTON, PASCAL K., and CAMPBELL, ARTHUR A. *Family Planning, Sterility and Population Growth*. New York: McGraw-Hill Book Co., 1959.

GIBBS, JACK P. (ed.). *Urban Research*. Princeton: D. Van Nostrand Company, 1961.

GINSBURG, NORMAN E. *Atlas of Economic Development*. Chicago: University of Chicago Press, 1961.

GLASS, D. V. (ed.). *Introduction to Malthus*. London: C. A. Watts and Company, 1953.

GLASS, D. V. and GREBENIK, E. *The Trend and Pattern of Fertility in Great Britain. A Report on the Family Census of 1946*, two volumes. (Papers of the Royal Commission on Population, Vol VI.) Part I, Report. Part II, Tables. London: H.M.S.O., 1954.

GLICK, PAUL C. *American Families*. New York: John Wiley and Sons, 1957.

GOTTMAN, JEAN. *Megalopolis: The Urbanized Northeastern Seaboard of the United States*. New York: The Twentieth Century Fund, 1961.

GRABILL, WILSON H., KISER, CLYDE V., and WHELPTON, PASCAL K. *The Fertility of American Women*. New York: John Wiley and Sons, 1958.

GREEP, ROY O. (ed.). *Human Fertility and Population Problems*. Cambridge: Schenkman Publishing Co., 1963.

GUTTMACHER, ALAN F. *The Complete Book of Birth Control*. New York: Ballantine Books, 1961.

HARTMAN, CARL G. *Science and the Safe Period*. Baltimore: The Williams Co., 1962.

HAUSER, PHILIP M. *Population Perspectives*. New Brunswick, New Jersey: Rutgers University Press, 1960.

———— (ed.). *Population and World Politics*. Glencoe, Illinois: The Free Press, 1958.

————. *The Population Explosion: World, National, Metropolitan*. New Brunswick, New Jersey: Rutgers University Press, 1960.

HAUSER, PHILIP M. and DUNCAN, OTIS DUDLEY (eds.). *The Study of Population*. Chicago: The University of Chicago Press, 1959.

HAWLEY, AMOS. *Human Ecology*. New York: Ronald Press, 1950.

HERTZLER, J. O. *The Crisis in World Population*. Lincoln, Nebraska: The University of Nebraska Press, 1956.

HIGBEE, EDWARD. *The Squeeze: Cities Without Space*. New York: William Morrow and Company, 1960.

HILL, REUBEN, STYCOS, J. MAYONE, and BACK, KURT W. *The Family and Population Control: A Puerto Rican Experiment in Social Change*. Chapel Hill: University of North Carolina Press, 1959.

HUXLEY, JULIAN. *New Bottles for New Wine*. New York: Harper and Brothers, 1957.

JACOBS, JANE. *The Death and Life of Great American Cities*. New York: Random House, 1961.

JACOBSON, PAUL H. *American Marriage and Divorce*. New York: Rinehart and Company, 1959.

JAFFE, ABRAM J. *People, Jobs and Economic Development: A Case History of Puerto Rico. Supplemented by Recent Mexican Experience*. Glencoe, Illinois: The Free Press, 1959.

JAFFE, A. J., and STEWART, CHARLES D. *Manpower Resources and Utilization*. New York: John Wiley and Sons, 1951.

JARRETT, HENRY (ed.). *Perspectives on Conservation: Essays on America's Natural Resources*. Baltimore: Johns Hopkins Press, 1958.

KELLY, GEORGE A. *Overpopulation: A Catholic View*. New York: Paulist Press, 1960.

KNAUS, HERMAN. *Human Procreation and Its Natural Regulation: How to Determine Accurately the Fertile and Sterile Days of the Menstrual Cycle*. New York: Ivan Obolensky, 1964 (New American Edition).

LIEBENSTEIN, HARVEY. *Economic Backwardness and Economic Growth*. New York: John Wiley and Sons, 1957.

LORIMER, FRANK, *et al. Culture and Human Fertility*. Paris: UNESCO, 1959.

MALTHUS, THOMAS, HUXLEY, JULIAN, and OSBORN, FREDERICK. *Three Essays on Population*. New York: Mentor Books, 1960.

MARSHALL, JOHN. *The Infertile Period*. Baltimore: Helicon, 1963.

McCORMACK, ARTHUR (ed.). *Christian Responsibility and World Poverty*. Westminster, Maryland: The Newman Press, 1963.

MEIER, RICHARD L. *Modern Science and the Human Fertility Problem*. New York: John Wiley and Sons, 1959.

———. *Science and Economic Development*. New York: Massachusetts Institute of Technology and John Wiley and Sons, 1956.

OKUN, BERNARD. *Trends in Birth Rates in the United States Since 1870*. Baltimore: Johns Hopkins Press, 1958.

ORDWAY, S. H. *Resources and the American Dream*. New York: Ronald Press, 1953.

OSBORN, FAIRFIELD. *Our Plundered Planet*. Boston: Little, Brown and Company. 1948.

OSBORN, FREDERICK (ed.). *Population: An International Dilemma*. New York: The Population Council, 1958.

——. *Preface to Eugenics*. Revised edition. New York: Harper and Brothers, 1951.

——. *This Crowded World*. (Public Affairs Pamphlet No. 306.) New York: Public Affairs Committee, December 1960.

PETERSEN, WILLIAM. *Population*. New York: MacMillan and Company, 1961.

PIDDINGTON, R. A. *The Limits of Mankind: A Philosophy of Population*. Bristol, England: John Wright and Sons, 1956.

RAINWATER, LEE. *And the Poor Get Children*. Chicago: Quadrangle Books, 1960.

ROBERTS, GEORGE W. *The Population of Jamaica*. Cambridge: Cambridge University Press, 1957.

ROCK, JOHN. *The Time Has Come*. New York: Avon Books, 1963.

ST. JOHN-STEVAS, NORMAN. *Birth Control and Public Policy*. Santa Barbara, California: Center for the Study of Democratic Institutions, 1960.

SAUVY, ALFRED. *Fertility and Survival: Population Problems from Malthus to Mao Tse-Tung*. New York: Criterion Books, 1961.

SAX, KARL. "The Population Explosion." *Headline Series #120*. New York: Foreign Policy Association, 1956.

——. *Standing Room Only*. Boston: Beacon Press, 1957.

SENIOR, CLARENCE. *Land Reform and Democracy*. Gainesville, Florida: University of Florida Press, 1958.

SHRYOCK, HENRY S., JR. *Population Mobility Within the United States*. Chicago: Community and Family Study Center, University of Chicago Press, 1964.

SPENGLER, JOSEPH J. (ed.). *Natural Resources and Economic Growth*. Washington, D. C.: Resources for the Future, 1961.

——. *Population Theory and Policy*. Glencoe, Illinois: The Free Press, 1956.

SPENGLER, JOSEPH J., and DUNCAN, OTIS DUDLEY (eds.). *Demographic Analysis: Selected Readings*. Glencoe, Illinois: The Free Press, 1956.

STALEY, EUGENE. *The Future of Underdeveloped Countries: Political Implications of Economic Development*. New York: Harper and Brothers, 1954.

STYCOS, J. MAYONE. *Family and Fertility in Puerto Rico*. New York: Columbia University Press, 1955.

SULLOWAY, ALVAH W. *Birth Control and Catholic Doctrine.* Boston: Beacon Press, 1959.

TAEUBER, CONRAD, and TAEUBER, IRENE. *The Changing Population of the United States.* New York: John Wiley and Sons, 1957.

TAEUBER, IRENE. *The Population of Japan.* Princeton: Princeton University Press, 1958.

TAFT, DONALD, and ROBBINS, RICHARD. *International Migrations.* New York: The Ronald Press, 1955.

THOMAS, DOROTHY SWAINE. *Research Memorandum on Migration Differentials.* (Bulletin 43.) New York: Social Science Research Council, 1938.

THOMAS, JOHN L. *Marriage and Rhythm.* Westminster, Maryland: The Newman Press, 1958.

THOMPSON, WARREN S. *Population Problems.* New York: McGraw-Hill Book Co., 1953.

————. *Population and Progress in the Far East.* Chicago: University of Chicago Press, 1959.

UNITED NATIONS. *Age and Sex Patterns of Mortality: Model Life-Tables for Underdeveloped Countries,* 1955, ST/SOA/Series A, No. 22.

————. *Demographic Yearbook.* Department of Economic and Social Affairs. New York. Published annually.

————. *Economic Characteristics of International Migrants: Statistics for Selected Countries, 1918–1954,* 1958, ST/SOA/Series A, No. 12; 58/XIII/3.

————. *Handbok of Population Census Methods,* 1954, ST/STAT/Series F, No. 5; 54/XVII/6.

————. *Handbook of Population Census Methods,* 1954, ST/STAT/Series F, No. 7; 55/XVII/1.

————. *Methods for Population Projections by Sex and Age,* 1956, ST/SOA/Series A, No. 25.

————. *Methods of Appraisal of Quality of Basic Date for Population Estimates,* 1955, ST/SOA/Series A, No. 23.

————. *Multilingual Demographic Dictionary* (in English), 1958, ST/SOA/Series A, No. 29; 58/XIII/4.

————. *Recent Trends in Fertility in Industrialized Countries,* 1958, ST/SOA/Series A, No. 27.

————. *Report on the World Social Situation: With Special Reference to the Problem of Balanced Social and Economic Development.* New York: 1961.

————. *The Aging of Populations and Its Economic and Social Implications,* 1956, ST/SOA/Series A, No. 26. 168 pp.

————. *The Future Growth of World Population*, 1958, ST/SOA/ Series A, No. 28; 58/XIII/2.

————. *The Determinants and Consequences of Population Trends*, 1953, ST/SOA/Series A, No. 17.

UNESCO. *The University Teaching of Social Sciences: Demography* (in English or in French), SS/57/VIII/9A. Paris: 1957. 200 pp.

VILLARD, HENRY H. *Economic Development*. New York: Rhine and Company, 1959.

VOGT, WILLIAM. *People: Challenge to Survival*. New York: William Sloane Associates, 1960.

WESTOFF, CHARLES F., *et al. Family Growth in Metropolitan America*. Princeton: Princeton University Press, 1963.

WHELPTON, P. K. *Cohort Fertility: Native-White Women in the United States*. Princeton: Princeton University Press, 1954.

WILLIAMS, GLANVILLE. *The Sanctity of Life and the Criminal Law*. New York: Alfred A. Knopf, 1957.

WILLIAMSON, HAROLD F., and BUTTRICK, JOHN A. (eds.). *Economic Development: Principles and Patterns*. New York: Prentice-Hall, 1954.

WRONG, DENNIS H. *Population and Society*. (Second revised and enlarged edition.) New York: Random House, 1962.

YAUKEY, DAVID. *Fertility Differences in a Modernizing Country: A Survey of Lebanese Couples*. Princeton University Press, 1961.

Articles

Duke University School of Law. "Population Control." *Law and Contemporary Problems*. Vol. 25, No. 3, Summer 1960. Durham, North Carolina: 1960. (Also, New York: Oceana Publications, 1961.)

Family Life Bureau, N.C.W.C. *Catholic Family Leader*, August 1963, pp. 2–3. *Reprint of American Bishops' Statement: June 1964*, pp. 2–3. *Excerpts from Letter of the then Cardinal Montini, 1963*.

National Bureau of Economic Research. "Demographic and Economic Change in Developed Countries." *Special Conference Series, No. 11*. Princeton: Princeton University Press, 1960.

Office of Population Research, Princeton University; and Population Association of America, Inc. *Population Index*. Published quarterly. (Indexes articles on many phases of population drawn from periodicals in the United States and abroad.)

Population Studies (London). Three issues annually.

Report, issue on population, June 1964.